GODARD AND OTHERS

FRONTISPIECE. *La Chinoise* (1967), directed by Jean-Luc Godard.

GODARD AND OTHERS
Essays on Film Form

Louis D. Giannetti

Rutherford • Madison • Teaneck
FAIRLEIGH DICKINSON UNIVERSITY PRESS
London: THE TANTIVY PRESS

© 1975 by Associated University Presses, Inc.

Associated University Presses, Inc.
Cranbury, New Jersey 08512

The Tantivy Press
108 New Bond Street
London W1Y OQX, England

Library of Congress Cataloging in Publication Data

Giannetti, Louis D
   Godard and others.

   Includes bibliographical references.
   1. Moving-pictures—Aesthetics.   I. Title.
PN1995.G48   791.43'01   73-2893
ISBN 0-8386-1291-1

PN
1995
.G48

SBN 0904208 30 3 (U.K.)
PRINTED IN THE UNITED STATES OF AMERICA

**For
JOHN HUNTLEY,
who taught me Aristotle**

CONTENTS

ACKNOWLEDGEMENTS		9
INTRODUCTION		13
1	Godard's *Masculine-Feminine:* The Cinematic Essay	19
2	The Aesthetic of the Mobile Camera	60
3	Cinematic Metaphors	89
4	*Alice's Restaurant* and the Tradition of the Plotless Film	132
INDEX		181

ACKNOWLEDGEMENTS

I would like to thank my friend and colleague, Walter Strauss, for the helpful suggestions he gave me on the Godard essay. I am indebted to Jonathan Benair and Jim Jeremias of the Larry Edmunds Book Shop, who helped me to locate many of the stills. Others who assisted me in finding stills are Dennis Gaughan, Al Vrabel, Steve Kotton, David Bell-Book, and especially Stefan Czapsky, formerly of the Case Western Reserve University Film Society.

I am particularly grateful to James Mason and Andrew Sarris for permission to quote from their works in *Interviews with Film Directors*. Two of these essays appeared, in much shorter versions, in the following publications: "*Alice's Restaurant* and the Tradition of the Plotless Film" in *The Western Humanities Review;* and "Cinematic Metaphors" in *The Journal of Aesthetic Education*.

I wish to thank the following publishers for having given me permission to quote from published works:

Charles Scribner's Sons, for permission to quote from Susanne Langer, *Feeling and Form*.
Crown Publishers, Inc., for permission to quote from "Interview with Jean-Luc Godard," in *Jean-Luc Godard,* 1970.
Doubleday & Company, Inc., for permission to quote from *Alice's Restaurant,* a Screenplay by Venable Herndon and Arthur Penn; and Richard Roud, *Godard*.

Grove Press, Inc., for permission to quote from *Masculine-Feminine,* edited by Pierre Billard and Robert Hughes, reprinted by permission of Grove Press, Inc., copyright © 1969 by Grove Press, Inc. All rights reserved.

Indiana University Press, for permission to quote from Robert Richardson, *Literature and Film.*

Newsweek, Inc., for permission to quote from "The New Movies," copyright *Newsweek,* Inc., 1970. Reprinted by permission.

The New York *Times* Company, for permission to quote from "The Question of Violence," by John Simon, © 1968-9 by the New York *Times* Company. Reprinted by permission.

Sight and Sound, for permission to quote from "Some Ideas on the Cinema," by Cesare Zavattini, and "Jean-Luc Godard and *Vivre Sa Vie,*" by Tom Milne. Reprinted by permission.

The University of California Press, for permission to quote from George Bluestone, *Novels into Film,* and *What is Cinema?* by André Bazin, translated by Hugh Gray. Orignally published by the University of California Press; reprinted by permission of the Regents of the University of California.

The Viking Press, Inc., for permission to quote from *Godard on Godard,* edited by Jean Narboni and Tom Milne. English translation Copyright © 1972 by Martin Secker & Warburg Ltd. Reprinted by permission of the Viking Press, Inc.

I wish to thank the following studios and distributing companies for the use of their publicity photos in this book:

Allied Artists, for *The Pawnbroker.*
Argosy Pictures-RKO, for *Wagonmaster.*
Arlan Pictures, Inc., for *The Earrings of Mme. de . . .*
Audio Brandon Films, for *Blood of a Poet, Umberto D, Bicycle Thief.*
Cinema V Distributing Inc., for *Accident, Elvira Madigan.*
Cinema Center, for *Little Big Man.*
Columbia Pictures, for *Macbeth, Hamlet, The Last Picture Show, Easy Rider, On the Waterfront, Mickey One, The Chase.*
Continental Films for *Faces, Grand Illusion.*
Embassy Pictures, for *Long Day's Journey Into Night.*
Films-Around-the-World, Inc., for *Breathless, Testament of Orpheus.*
Grove Press, for *Weekend.*
Janus Films for *Jules and Jim, Beauty and the Beast, La Ronde, L'Avventura, Rules of the Game, The Seventh Seal.*
Jay Ward Productions, Inc., for *The General.*
Kingsley International Pictures Corp., for *Le Plaisir.*

Acknowledgements

Leacock Pennebaker, Inc., for *La Chinoise*.
Mayer & Burstyn, for *Paisan*.
MGM, for *The Navigator, North by Northwest, Zabriskie Point*.
Museum of Modern Art, for *Intolerance, The Musketeers of Pig Alley*.
New Yorker Films, for *Before the Revolution*.
Paramount Pictures, for *Monte Carlo, The Scarlet Empress, Blonde Venus, Psycho, Nanook of the North*.
Pathe Cinema, for *My Life to Live*.
Pathe-Contemporary, for *Pierrot Le Fou, Open City*.
Rizzoli Fillms, for *Juliet of the Spirits*.
RKO, for *Notorious*.
Royal Films International, for *Masculine-Feminine*.
Toho Productions, for *Ikiru*.
TransAmerica Releasing Corp., for *The Sins of Lola Montès*.
20th Century Fox, for *Man Hunt*.
United Artists, for *Scarface, The African Queen, Alice's Restaurant, Paths of Glory, The Hospital, The Shame, The Passion of Anna, The Miracle Worker, Stolen Kisses*.
Universal International, for *The Birds*.
Wanger-United Artists, for *Stagecoach*.
Warner Brothers, for *A Clockwork Orange, Deliverance, Key Largo, Bonnie and Clyde*.

INTRODUCTION

To me, style is just the outside of content, and content the inside of style, like the outside and inside of the human body—both go together, they can't be separated.

—Jean-Luc Godard

By and large, film criticism has been content-oriented. Most of what we read about the movies could just as easily be about novels or plays as about films. In some cases, this is apparently due to sheer ignorance: a surprising number of reviewers and critics are simply insensitive to cinematic form. To them, movies are "stories." Other critics—even good ones, like Pauline Kael—seem to believe that discussions of form or technique are rather pedantic, even decadent. Critics of Miss Kael's calibre are perfectly aware of the technical aspects of movies but seldom bother to *comment* on cinematic form, other than a few general remarks about the photography or the editing. Criticism of this sort often seems arbitrary (and even, on occasion, mystical), for we never see specifically *how* the writer arrives at his conclusions. "Content" is postulated as an independent entity, and not as an expression of "form."

At the other end of the spectrum are those critics—like Raymond Durgnat—who insist, in theory if not always in practice, that form and content are the same. Influenced no doubt by the New Criticism in literature, such commentators point out that the "content" of an art work such as a novel in any other "form" (e.g., an outline or paraphrase) is no longer the real content. Durgnat and others have pointed out that most film critics discuss content only in this crude subject-matter sense. But if this were a valid conception, we ought logically to conclude that there is no significant difference between Laurence Olivier's filmed *Hamlet* and Tony Richardson's movie of the same work; or, for that matter, between *any* film version and the play, since the "content" is the same. But of course there are enormous differences between these two excellent films, largely because of the differences in form.

What's involved here is an old—and perhaps tedious—problem. Certainly all critics are forced to discuss form and content separately on occasion. The form-content division in movies is not so simple as it is in music or non-representational painting, where in effect there is no content except the "pure form." Furthermore, in some very important respects, content *is* a detachable entity, at least with some works of art, otherwise the genius of, for instance, Dostoievsky's *Crime and Punishment,* would not be apparent in translation, for a translation is no longer its true form.

To insist therefore, that all great movies are great by virtue of their form alone is a shaky premise. As a director, Chaplin is often a clumsy technician. His genius consists of what he does *before* the camera as an actor, and seldom what he does *with* it as a *metteur-en-scène*. A film directed by Chaplin without Chaplin the actor is not likely to be a great or even good work, as *A Countess from Hong Kong* sadly revealed. Furthermore, most of Chaplin's great acting scenes would be just as effective in the legitimate theater as in film, perhaps even more so. Brilliance of directorial technique is not always a reliable gauge of artistic excellence in film. As in the other arts, there are many gifted technical directors in the cinema—Douglas Sirk, Jerry Lewis, Sergio Leone—who are hardly great artists. Their technical skills, for the most part, are used merely to "dress up" the poverty of inspiration in their subject matter, to make the *clichés* more palatable.

Josef von Sternberg, a great film technician, used to boast that story content was of no interest to him whatsoever. "Pure form" was his concern in his films. Yet Sternberg's masterpieces are those films that welded form with significant subject matter—*The Blue Angel, The Scarlet Empress,* and *The Saga of Anatahan.* For the most part, his exercises in "pure form"—movies like the empty *Devil Is a Woman*—look pretty campy today. For all their visual opulence, these films are ultimately trivial and decadent. In short, there are too many crude geniuses who manage to produce masterpieces and too many facile technicians who produce only clever trifles for us to insist without qualification on the inseparability of form and content.

But if Durgnat and the other formalists are not completely persuasive, their insistence on the necessity of dicussing technique in film criticism is long overdue. How a director says something may not be

Introduction

exactly the same thing as what he says, but for too long, critics have glibly discussed the whats of movies without even bothering about the hows and whys. Not all critics are guilty of this belletristic vagueness. Stephen Farber, Robin Wood, David Bordwell, and Charles Barr, among others, have done much to bring the form-content relationship back into balance. Hopefully, the following essays will be a modest addition to their achievements.

Each of these four essays is concerned with cinematic form, or the technical means by which ideas and emotions are expressed in movies. Two of the essays, *"Alice's Restaurant* and the Tradition of the Plotless Film"and "Godard's *Masculine-Feminine:* The Cinematic Essay," deal primarily with film structures, or how various details relate to a unified whole. The other two essays, "Cinematic Metaphors" and "The Aesthetic of the Mobile Camera," deal with film texture, or how individual techniques can be used to convey specific ideas within a variety of contexts. My assumption throughout this study has been that the best method of determining what these directors have to say is to analyse and explore the implications of how they say it.

Every film technique has its own implied aesthetic. When a shot from a film doesn't "work," it's often because the ideas or feelings behind the shot are inadequately expressed. Or simply, the "content" of the shot is not sufficiently fused with, or embodied by its "form." From a strictly practical standpoint, we can look at a technique merely as a means to an end, as a specific *manner* of expressing something . This implies that there may be several equally appropriate ways of saying the same thing.

For example, if a director wished to express a character's social insignificance, there are a number of methods open to him. The character's unimportance could be conveyed simply through dialogue—the literary solution. Or a director might exploit his *mise-en-scène* and place the character low on the frame, or at the edges of the frame—those areas that intrinsically tend to suggest insignificance. Another film-maker might prefer a close-up of his actor, who would convey this idea histrionically. Still another solution would be to use a high angle shot of the actor, thus forcing the audience to "look down" on the character.

Since each of these methods implies a different aesthetic response, it stands to reason that the "content" is also going to be different in some subtle way, though the *general* idea of insignificance could probably be expressed through all of these techniques. We usually admire a shot because it seems inescapably "right" in some way. This sense of inevitability is due in large part to a director's technical fastidiousness.

A good director might choose any of the above solutions to convey the of idea social insignificance, but the great director is great by virtue of the justness and precision of his choice. I am not suggesting that there is any absolute technique for every idea and emotion—though this can often seem to be the case in retrospect. What I do suggest is that a reliable gauge of genius in a film-maker is the degree to which his forms or techniques seem undetachable from the ideas and emotions they express.

As we have seen, there are a number of techniques at a director's disposal for conveying the general idea of insignificance. But of course, context is all. Some of these techniques suggest nuances of meaning that could conflict in subtle ways with the precise ideas that the film-maker is trying to embody. The literary solution—perhaps the easiest—would involve the problem of self-consciousness. Would the character be likely to admit to his own sense of insignificance? Or if another character were to comment on it, would *he* be likely to speak openly? Furthermore, a shot of the second character is likely to shift our attention away from our original concern. The *mise-en-scène* solution would invariably involve a comparison or contrast with other people and objects in the frame, elements which might conflict with the ideas the director wants to include. And so on, with each of the other alternatives.

In short, the great director selects his techniques with as much concern for nuance as the poet in choosing his words. I am not suggesting that all directors manipulate their shots with painstaking self-consciousness. Indeed, with the exception of film-makers like Hitchcock and Eisenstein (who have explained their choice of techniques in detail), I would guess that most film directors are intuitive about such matters. Nor should this necessarily be otherwise. An artist's job is creation: how he goes about it is his own business. On the other hand, explication—or *why* an artist makes certain choices, and why these choices are so effective—is the critic's province.

Ultimately, a director's choice of techniques takes us into the realm of style, which inevitably leads us to matters of an artist's "vision." For example, certain film-makers tend to avoid the mobile camera. They might argue that this technique is too expensive, too clumsy, too time consuming; or, like John Ford, they might simply claim that they dislike it. The predominance of a stable camera in Ford's work is more than just an arbitrary matter of style, however, for stationary set-ups tend to imply a certain personal vision of the world, one involving stability, permanence, even stolidity. Technique, in this case, is style. And a director's style tells us a good deal about his philosophical and ethical values. Technique, in short, is content. Or at least a very basic component of content.

GODARD AND OTHERS

1
Godard's *Masculine-Feminine*: The Cinematic Essay

I consider myself an essayist; I do essays in the form of novels and novels in the form of essays: simply, I film them instead of writing them.

Film is like a personal diary, a notebook or a monologue by someone who tries to justify himself before a camera.

Movies are a world of fragments.

I don't know how to tell stories. I want to cover the whole ground, from all possible angles, saying everything at once.

Of course, it is my secret ambition to be put in charge of French newsreels. Each of my films constitutes a report on the state of the nation: they are news reportages, treated in a quirkish way perhaps, but rooted in actuality.

I

All of the above statements were made by Jean-Luc Godard during various interviews. The blend of whimsy, self-mockery, perverseness, and earnestness is a perfect reflection of his technique of film-making. More than any other contemporary director, Godard has been the subject of a bitter and often tiresome controversy. His detractors view his films with suspicious hostility at best, and at worst, with furious indignation. For example, in a New York *Times* article, John Simon dismisses Godard's entire *oeuvre:*

> In the films of Jean-Luc Godard there is no respect for anything: meaning, communication, significant form, men, women, or life. There is no respect even for what has distinguished most previous avant-garde movements: rebellion in the name of greater freedom. Godard's rebellion is just for the sake of infantile self-indulgence. In his work there is no affection that does not reek of affectation, no jest that is not merely a rude gesture, no movement that has motivation as well as motion to it....Godard clearly does not have the faintest idea where he is going with his scene, his film, his oeuvre——so he blithely goes off in all directions simultaneously. It is an act of consummate pretentiousness, irresponsible violence, and vacuity.[1]

Other critics look upon Godard as one of the few genuinely relevant film-makers of our time. Interestingly enough, his most enthusiastic champions and detractors often single out the same characteristics in support of their views. Susan Sontag, for example, praises Godard's *My Life to Live*[2] *(Vivre sa vie)* as a "nearly perfect work," not despite its clumsy acting, its sterile intellectuality, its talkiness, and its shallow characterization, but virtually *because* of these characteristics (fig. 1). Everyone seems to agree that Godard's films are unique. The problem revolves around whether this uniqueness is good or bad.

Those who dislike his movies generally complain of the lack of coherence in his narratives. The absence of plot is common enough in documentary films, but Godard's movies are neither documentaries nor fiction films in the strict sense of either term. Many of his movies cut across *genre* distinctions, combining documentary realism, stylised tableaux, propaganda, whimsical digressions on art, culture, and sociology in a bizarre and often bewildering mixture. Like most experimental artists, Godard likes to push his techinques to the precipice of incoherence: he is constantly flirting with chaos. Sometimes these flirtations result in banal disasters, like *Alphaville* or *See You at Mao*. When he miraculously pulls it off, as in *Masculine-Feminine (Masculin-Féminin), La Chinoise,* and much of *Weekend* and *Vladimir and Rosa (Vladimir und Rosa),* he astonishes us with the

---

1. "The Question of Violence," quoted in *Jean-Luc Godard: An Investigation into His Films and Philosophy,* edited by Jean Collet (New York: Crown Publishers, Inc., 1970), pp. 161-62.
2. "Godard's *Vivre Sa Vie,*" in *Against Interpretation* (New York: A Delta Book, 1966).

FIG. 1. *My Life to Live* (1962), directed by Jean-Luc Godard. Influenced by the films of Carl Dreyer, the Danish director, *My Life to Live* is in many respects a "woman's film," employing the metaphor of prostitution as an analogue of contemporary capitalism. Anna Karina (shown here) plays Nana, the central character.

richness and complexity of his approach.

A number of hostile commentators have interpreted Godard's rejection of plot as a tacit recognition on his part that he simply lacks a narrative gift. There may be some truth to this view, though more likely his rejection is based primarily on philosophical considerations.

Throughout his career, Godard has expressed great admiration for American *genre* films, especially those of Hitchcock, Lang, and Hawks. What he particularly likes about their movies is their plots. Godard's first feature, *Breathless (A bout de souffle,* 1959) is partially indebted to these tightly-structured *genre* films, though more in terms of textural details than structure, for the plot of *Breathless* is rather rambling compared to most American thrillers (fig. 2).

FIG. 2. *Breathless* (1959), directed by Jean-Luc Godard. Like most of his early works, Godard's first feature was strongly indebted to American *genre* films, in this case, Howard Hawks's gangster classic, *Scarface*. Pictured above, Jean-Paul Belmondo and Jean Seberg as the two prinicipals.

Godard's Masculine-Feminine: The Cinematic Essay

What Godard recognises about the nature of tight narrative structures is the air of inevitability they seem to suggest. A good plot generally avoids coincidences, inconsistencies, and too many surprises. Everything must fit into an overall design, including what the characters say and do. In short, there's a certain degree of predictability which we value in a well-plotted tale. Once the artist establishes his premises, we don't take favorably to any "cheating," even if it provides some momentary excitement. If coincidences, inconsistencies, and surprises are used, they must seem "logical," at least in retrospect.[3]

Film-makers whose artistic vision is essentially pessimistic have been attracted to *genre* films as vehicles. Many of Fritz Lang's works, for example, deal with the idea of fate or predestination (fig. 3). In *You*

FIG. 3. *Man Hunt* (1941), directed by Fritz Lang. Several of Godard's early movies, like the films of Lang, feature a protagonist on the run, yet unable, ultimately, to escape his destiny.

---

3. For a more detailed discussion of these and related ideas, see Section I of "Alice's *Restaurant* and the Tradition of the Plotless Film," below.

Only Live Once, Lang's plot is carefully constructed to show how the protagonist is a victim of forces beyond his control, forces he does not even realise are at work in determining his destiny. Hitchcock also manipulates his plots to suggest the inexorability of fate and the feeble helplessness of men who are trapped by the forces of circumstances (figs. 4,5). Both Hitchcock and Lang tend to view such notions as self-determination and the efficacy of the will as delusions. For Lang, these delusions are tragic and often ennobling; for Hitchcock, they are absurd and grimly comical.

There was obviously something about these pessimistic views that attracted Godard, for in many of his films, his protagonists model themselves on characters from American *genre* movies. Perhaps, as Pauline Kael has suggested, it's the cool invulnerability of the American prototypes that appeals to Godard's characters, especially the youthful ones. But as an Existential Marxist, committed to the efficacy and freedom of the will, to the viability of social revolution, and the

FIG. 4. *The Birds* (1963), directed by Alfred Hitchcock. An early enthusiast of Hitchcock's work, Godard once observed "People say that Hitchcock lets the wires show too often. But because he shows them they are no longer wires. They are the pillars of a marvellous architectural design made to withstand our scrutiny."

FIG. 5. *Weekend* (1968), directed by Jean-Luc Godard. Even after his feelings towards the U.S.A. had hardened into hatred, Godard continued to be influenced by the American cinema. *Weekend,* like the works of Hitchcock, is filled with bizarre, unpredictable outbursts of violence in everyday life, outbursts that are often as funny as they are unnerving.

necessity of overcoming imposed obstacles, Godard ultimately had to reject determinism and all it implied. Gradually, he came to place less and less emphasis on plots, and more on improvisation, probably for these philosophical and political reasons.

For several years, Godard experimented with alternate cinematic structures, sometimes successfully, often not. With amazing rapidity, he turned out an average of two movies a year, some of them employing radically experimental techiques (fig. 6). Perhaps none of his films of the early Sixties is completely satisfying, and some of them are terrible. Certainly no other major film director is so uneven artistically as Godard, but even his worst movies contain a few interesting shots or a brilliant sequence or two. Eventually, he came to repudiate these early "bourgeois" films—movies like *Breathless, My Life to Live,* and *Contempt (Le mépris)* in which Fritz Lang played himself—as ideologically unsound. More plotted than his later works, some of these early

FIG. 6. *Pierrot le fou* (1965), directed by Jean-Luc Godard. Shot in widescreen and brilliant color, *Pierrot le fou* blended elements from the allegories of brutalism of Samuel Fuller, the gangster films of Fritz Lang, and the lush lyricism of Renoir's most romantic films of the fifties.

films deal with the triumph of fate over the individual.

While working on *Masculine-Feminine* in 1965, Godard managed to consolidate most of the piecemeal triumphs of his earlier movies. The film is a masterpiece of eclecticism, uniting a wide range of techniques in a totally new kind of structure. The cinematic essay had at last come into its own. "Essay" is Godard's own term, and he uses it in Montaigne's original sense of an attempt, a search of some kind. The discursive freedom found in the literary essays of Montaigne provided Godard with a structural counterpart for the kind of movies he wanted to make. An essay is neither fiction nor fact, but a personal investigation involving both the passion and intellect of the author. Traditionally, there have been three broad categories of movies: experimental films, fiction, and documentaries. Godard had to invent a fourth. His cinematic essays are in a sense a highly personalised mixture of the three traditional categories, in addition to those "little things" he delights in including for good measure.

Though he acknowledges and respects that view of film-making —best represented by Eisenstein and Hitchcock—which emphasises pre-planning and precision of execution, Godard prefers and works best with a looser, more improvisatory approach. He thinks the best movies are those in which the director conducts a dialectical search, experimenting and discovering his theme and structure as he goes along. This partly explains his incredible diversity, for he dislikes repeating himself: "I prefer to look for something I don't know, rather than be able to do better with something I do know."[4]

His approach involves great artistic dangers, for Godard is not always sure of what he will discover during his investigations. Sometimes what he finds isn't particularly worth preserving. In a sense, the plot to a thriller is also a kind of search—the classic "who dunnit?" But Godard's investigations are not so specific. He tackles more general and philosophical subjects—usually involving sex or politics, often both. In *Masculine-Feminine*, for example, he attempts to discover the nature of contemporary French youth: What are their problems, their ideals, their lifestyles? What do they read, and what movies do they like (fig. 7)? What do they think about political issues? What's their sex life like? And so on.

These questions inevitably suggest the documentary, and particularly *cinéma-vérité*, with its emphasis on interviews and political and sociological subjects. Godard has been influenced by *cinéma-vérité* (there are five interviews in *Masculine-Feminine*), but he finds its style rather dry and pedantic, especially as practiced in America. Furthermore, he scoffs at its pretence to objectivity. In discussing Richard Leacock, the American *cinéma-vérité* documentarist, Godard criticised the lack of commitment, the "moral vacuum" of many of Leacock's films:

> There's no point in having sharp images if you've got fuzzy ideas. Leacock's lack of subjectivity leads him ultimately to a lack of *objectivity*. He doesn't even know that he is a *metteur-en-scène*, that pure reportage doesn't exist.[5]

Godard's cinematic essays have also been influenced by the plays of Bertolt Brecht. Like Godard, Brecht insisted that the artist must be overtly didactic, that he must inculcate moral and political (i.e., Marxist) lessons. From Brecht, Godard borrowed the famous "alienation

---

4. Quoted in *Godard on Godard,* edited by Jean Narboni and Tom Milne (New York: The Viking Press, 1972), p. 186.

5. Quoted by Richard Roud, *Godard* (New York: Doubleday & Company, Inc., 1968), p. 139.

FIG. 7. *Masculine-Feminine* (1965), directed by Jean-Luc Godard. Godard's films are often criticised for their "pretentious" quotations from novels, plays, films, even songs. In response, Godard has said: "People in life quote as they please, so we have the right to quote as we please. Therefore I show people quoting, merely making sure that they quote what pleases me."

effect," or the emotional endistancing of the audience from the action and characters. Only if the viewer is not totally absorbed by the action can he evaluate rationally the ideological implications of what he has witnessed. Emotional identification is not denied, but carefully controlled through a number of techniques. One of the most important of these is a de-emphasis of plot. Theoretically, Brecht's plays are unified not by the interaction of character and incident in a cause-effect pattern, but simply by the presence of a central character, or by a static situation. He believed that each scene exists as an independent unit—a playlet, as it were. These scenes are loosely strung together in a sequence, but the sequence is relatively arbitrary. Presumably, any unit could be lifted from its position in the play and shifted to another position without any significant alteration in meaning.

There has always been some question as to whether Brecht's practice was in accord with his theory, particularly in his best plays. But these techniques work admirably in Godard's cinematic essays, perhaps because of the nature of the medium. Movies, as Godard has reminded us, are a world of fragments—bits and pieces of celluloid are literally spliced together. Even in conventional films time and space are chopped up and reassembled into a new continuity. Godard simply carries this process several steps further by intercutting a wider assortment of fragments. Since he used no real plots in his essays, narrative continuity is no problem, and hence, he is free to assemble his units along other lines.

II

Masculine-Feminine is constructed in terms of a number of polarities, most of them sexual and political. The central character, Paul, is a likable, rather naive young Communist whose political philosophy finds expression primarily in conversations. He also carries with him an aerosol can of paint which he uses to write anti-capitalist and anti-American slogans on walls and cars. Like many of Godard's heroes Paul is a searcher constantly groping to define and understand himself, trying to achieve stability in a chaotic environment. Robert, Paul's friend, is a factory worker and also a Communist, though far more committed to the Party, and personally more self-confident than Paul. Godard's two masculine characters are obsessed with two topics: sex and politics. Throughout the film, they are constantly horny and constantly frustrated by the political realities of the times. (The film is set in Paris, late in 1965, between elections. Later, De Gaulle went on to win the elections. At the same time the American war was rapidly escalating in Vietnam.)

There are also three young women in the film: Madeleine, a rising pop singer whom Paul has fallen in love with, and Catherine and Elisabeth, her friends. Catherine is attracted to Paul, but he has eyes only for Madeleine, who seems to have eyes only for herself. To complicate matters, Robert is attracted to Catherine, who is only vaguely interested in him. Elisabeth is not much developed as a character, though there is a hint of lesbianism in her relationship with Madeleine.[6] The young women also think about sex a lot, but none of

---

6. The film is based—very loosely—on two Maupassant stories, "Paul's Girl," which concerns a young man in love with a girl he fears is a lesbian, and "The Signal," upon which the "Swedish film" within the film is based.

them is really interested in politics. Throughout the film, Godard associates the female principle with consumer goods, capitalism, and the physical world, as opposed to the somewhat more idealistic preoccupations of the males. In general, the girls are more practical, more autonomous, and more concerned with self.

Although a great deal takes place in the movie, the events seem random and detached. Certainly there is little resembling a conventional plot: Paul meets Madeleine and asks if she can help him get a job with a magazine she works for, *Mademoiselle 19 Ans*. We are never shown how he gets the job, but the next time we see him, he's working for the magazine. Paul tries to go to bed with Madeleine, but though they eventually become lovers, Godard never shows us their initial sexual encounter. Later in the film, Paul takes a job with the IFOP, a government bureau that gauges public opinion. Madeleine meanwhile achieves some modest fame as a singer. Lest we become too involved with the "plot," Godard doesn't even show us Paul's death at the end

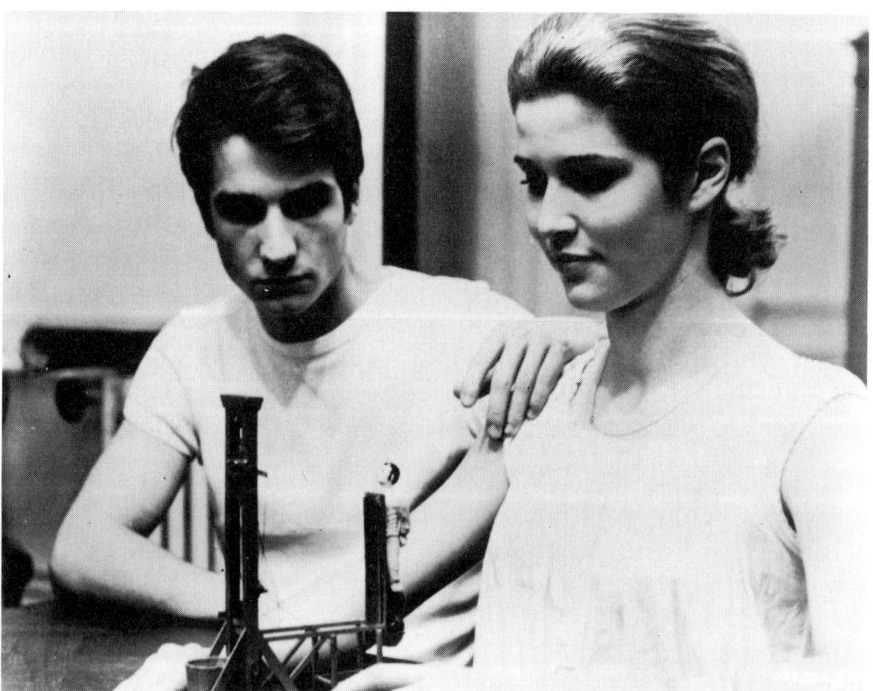

FIG. 8. *Masculine-Feminine*. Catherine (Catherine-Isabelle Duport) is the most likable of the three females in Godard's film but even she seems to have a subtle attraction to violence, as can be seen in the episode where she demonstrates to Paul (Jean-Pierre Léaud) how a male doll is decapitated by a toy guillotine.

of the film. We're merely informed that he fell from a window, probably accidentally, though there is a hint of suicide.

Within this loose structure, Godard is able to develop an extraordinary range of themes: the pain and transience of love, the self-destructive effects of sexuality, the futility of genuine communication, the impenetrable mysteries of the human personality, the pathos of loneliness, the alienating depersonalisation of the city, the necessity for social commitment and personal identity, the debasement of culture, and the coarsening effects of contemporary capitalism. In short, the movie is a perfect illustration of what Godard self-mockingly alludes to as "my passion for analysing what is called modern life."

What differentiates Godard from other, more conventional Marxist film-makers is the profound sense of ambivalence that suffuses his movie. Logically, Paul should be attracted to the softer, more intellectual Catherine, rather than to Madeleine, who is the most shallow of the three girls (fig. 8). Madeleine is obsessed with the "success" ethic: indeed, she is the film's most prominent exemplar of capitalism. Paul's

FIG. 9. *Masculine-Feminine*. Throughout the film, Paul is impressed by the Marxist orthodoxy of his friend Robert (Michael Debord), who is as cocksure and confident as Paul is stumbling and uncertain.

love for her makes no sense ideologically. But that is Godard's point: since she *is* a symbol of capitalism, Paul's irrational attraction to her represents an ideological paradox as well as a personal one. Robert criticises Paul for his political amateurism: an "individual solution" to capitalism is not possible, according to the more orthodox Robert. Paul agrees, and expresses admiration for Robert's commitment to the Party, yet is unable to go the length himself (fig. 9). Throughout the film, Paul—like Godard—is nagged by doubts and self-doubts. Commitment, both personal and political, is always difficult, always qualified.[7]

This sense of ambiguity and ambivalence also extends to Godard's treatment of the women. Despite Madeleine's rather phony cuteness, for example, she is capable of surprising us, especially in moments of repose. In shot after shot, Godard keeps her under exclusive surveillance, almost as though he believes that the sheer duration of these close-ups will reveal a hidden dimension of sensitivity. Astonishingly, sometimes these candid shots *do* reveal something—a sense of mystery, a depth of expression that we would never have expected. In one scene for example, she casually prepares to go to bed with Paul. When the lights are out, she grows pensive, her face acquiring a melancholy thoughtfulness (fig. 10). As Paul embraces her, she tenderly recites a poem on the solitude of men and the painful consolations of love against death. This—from tough, shrewd little Madeleine! The recital of the poem is totally "out of character," yet it has all the authenticity of those paradoxes of life that drive people like Godard mad with exasperation. Precisely because one is not expecting such things from Madeleine, we sympathise with Paul's dilemma. She is certainly shallow—but then. . . . Some critics angrily cite such scenes as typical examples of Godard's "perverseness." Why go to the trouble of establishing a character only to demolish it with one of these "inconsistant" strokes, they argue? Or if the character "really" changes, why does she revert to her old self in the following scenes? Perhaps we've all been debauched by conventional notions of "characterisation." Like Hitchcock, Godard sets out to shake our complacency. Throughout the movie, he assaults our *clichés* and preconceptions of human behavior, he does not permit us to relax, but forces us to make evaluations, to adjust or correct them, even to start over again if necessary. In short, his audiences must "search" for the truth just as he and his characters must.

---

7. Much of Godard's most recent work is totally committed to Maoism. Predictably, the films tend to lack the ambivalence and ambiguity of his previous works. See especially the blatantly crude and propagandist *See You at Mao*.

FIG. 10. *Masculine-Feminine*. One of the rare instances of serenity and mutual tenderness in the film. Paul and Madeleine (Chantal Goya) are in bed—which is also shared by Elisabeth. Unpredictably, the insensitive Madeleine recites a touching poem on the solitude of men.

Godard has an instinctive skepticism towards artistic neatness: he demonstrates the inadequacies of stereotyped, inflexible responses. Audiences prefer the security of knowing where they stand, a view shared by many critics. But Godard works dialectically. He is too honest—at least in this film—to warp the facts to fit a thesis. He presents one side of an issue, then its opposite, then another side, and so on. This refining dialectic continues to the very end of the movie, and even beyond that point the process could go on. (Godard has referred to his individual movies as "chapters" of a continuing investigation.) For people who like their films clear-cut and definitive, works like *Masculine-Feminine* are bound to produce a sense of frustration.

Godard has been condemned for his habit of "dragging in" gratuitous episodes. Many of his scenes are set in public places (cafés, arcades, laundromats, streets), and at times he seems to let the camera wander off randomly. But a closer analysis usually reveals that these "gratuitous" scenes are actually variations or parallels to his major theme. For example, *Masculine-Feminine* is saturated with violence and killing. In the very opening scene, when Paul first meets Madeleine in a café, a husband and wife can be heard quarreling. He walks out in a fury, pursued by his wife. Paul's only response is to yell at her to shut the door. On the busy street, before her young son, the woman shoots her husband. Godard does not pursue the episode between the man and his wife—it's offered as an example of the casual violence that takes place everywhere in the world of the film. Indeed, what makes the scene so appalling is its grotesque matter-of-factness.

In another café scene later in the film, we see the woman again, hustling a German laborer. (The theme of prostitution is common in Godard's work and is often used as a symbol of capitalism.) In the same café, the youngsters see Brigitte Bardot, being coached by her manager. At first we are inclined to think that this time, Godard has really gone too far. How can he "explain" the presence of Bardot? But the brief scene is clearly related to his major theme. Madeleine is particulary fascinated with the sex goddess, and watches her with rapt attention. "BB" is the incarnation of everything that Madeleine

FIG. 11. *Masculine-Feminine*. In one curiously mysterious sequence, an unknown young woman (a call girl?), rigid and melancholy, is escorted into the American Embassy by an Army officer.

Godard's Masculine-Feminine: *The Cinematic Essay* 35

wishes to become: a glamorous celebrity, with one of the highest priced bodies in the world (fig. 11). She is a commercial product, and her conversation with her manager revolves around the problem of how to package this product more attractively.

An important variation takes the form of a sick joke. Catherine and Paul are walking along the street when a strange man approaches them and asks Paul for some matches. The youth gives him some, and the stranger walks off, to Paul's consternation. While Catherine waits, Paul goes off to retrieve his matches. When he returns, he is visibly shaken. He tells Catherine that the man said goodbye to his wife, walked to the American hospital, doused himself with gasoline, and set himself on fire. The message he left to the world was: "Peace in Vietnam." Like a previous suicide in the film (fig. 12), this brief excursion into black humor is offered perhaps as a forshadowing of Paul's own death at the end of the film. (In all, there are at least four, and possibly six people killed in the movie, all of them males.)

Grim as some of these scenes are, the film is also very funny, which

FIG. 12. *Masculine-Feminine*. A bizzare episode from the arcade sequence. Without warning, Paul is threatened by a stranger brandishing a knife. Suddenly—gratuitously—he turns the knife on himself and collapses on the ground, dead.

is typical of most of Godard's work. Even in *Breathless,* he had developed his technique of alternating comedy with tragedy, and sometimes combining them simultaneously. In referring to one of his early movies, *A Woman Is a Woman (Une femme est une femme)* Godard said:

> I meant it to be contradictory, juxtaposing things which didn't necessarily go together, a film which was gay and sad at the same time. One can't do that, of course, one must be either one or the other, but I wanted to be both at once.[8]

In *Masculine-Feminine* too, many of the scenes are simultaneously serious and laughable. Godard has a genius for capturing that peculiarly phony way youngsters can behave when they think they're being most sincere. For example, in the scene where Paul and Madeleine meet for the first time, she casually asks him what it was like to be in the army. He gravely recounts the lack of freedom, leisure, and love. "In other words," he concludes, "modern life." The only response that the more prosaic Madeleine can offer is, "Yes, it doesn't sound like much fun." Throughout the film, Madeleine is a perfect foil to Paul's rather pompous solemnity. The contrast is usually amusing — and sad.

This contrasting technique is particularly effective in the various interview scenes, where Godard often rivets his camera on the subject, while questions are asked off-screen. A great deal of ambiguity is created by the tension between the spoken language, which is usually evasive or neutral, and the facial expressions and actions of the persons interviewed. Many of these scenes are photographed in long takes. In the first interview, for example, the shots average over a minute in length. Paul and Madeleine are in a washroom of the magazine office (fig. 13). As he questions her—about her interests, her love life, and her goals—Godard keeps the camera (in medium close-up) primarily on her. During most of the interview, she primps before a mirror, smoothing her hair, correcting her make-up, staring provocatively at Paul, fluffing her hair, recorrecting her make-up, and so on. Paul tries hard to stay cool, yet he cannot help but betray his vulnerabilities. Then comes her turn to ask questions: she asks why he wants to take her out. With touching guilelessness, he replies, "Because of tenderness." She's intrigued. "Without affection," he adds simply, "you might as well shoot yourself." The thought had obvi-

---

8. Quoted in "Jean Luc Godard and *Vivre Sa Vie,*" an interview by Tom Milne, in *Jean-Luc Godard,* edited by Toby Mussman (New York: E.P. Dutton & Co., Inc., 1968), p. 84.

Godard's Masculine-Feminine: *The Cinematic Essay*

FIG. 13. *Masculine-Feminine*. The washroom sequence between Madeleine and Paul. Composed of a series of interviews, this scene is photographed mostly in close-ups. This shot is one of the rare instances where both of them share the same frame.

ously never entered her mind. In a more philosophical vein, she asks. "What is the center of your world?" After some embarrassment, he responds, "Love, I guess." In one of those surprising flashes of candor, she observes, "That's funny, I would have answered—me."

In many respects, this scene can be viewed as a microcosm of the entire movie. Paul's need for affection and love is broadly political as well as personal. His idealistic but rather theoretical commitment to Marxism is motivated by the same need for "tenderness" as his commitment to Madeleine. Yet he's also inured somewhat to the callousness of most of the people he meets—how could he be otherwise in a world steeped in violence and casual cruelty? ("This was the era of James Bond and Vietnam," Paul observes in one of his voice-over monologues.) Madeleine is far less vulnerable: since her world centers on herself, she is not dependent upon others. She likes sex, but doesn't need—nor probably want—love. To her, the outside world is an arena for self-aggrandisement. Paul is interesting to have around, but "he mustn't become a bore." In a dialogue between the two men later in the film, Robert observes that in the (French) word "masculine" there is both "mask" and "ass." When Paul asks what's in feminine, Robert answers, "nothing." Godard gives this word-play a grim comical twist at the end of the film. Madeleine is at the police station, offering her version of Paul's death. When the questioning officer asks what she's going to do about her pregnancy, she fingers her hair prettily and sighs, "I don't know." She looks away, waits a few moments, then, with wide-eyed girlishness, says "I'm not sure." Godard then concludes his film with the quick title: FEMININE. A piercing gun shot rings out, and the "wounded" title now reads: F   IN . There was something in "feminine" after all.

Throughout the movie, Paul asks questions, observes behavior, and tries to formulate General Truths. His job as a pollster with the French Institute of Public Opinion is analogous in many ways to Godard's conception of film-making as an investigation of contemporary life. Both men discover that the truth is elusive and ambiguous. In one of those extraordinary *tour-de-force* scenes for which he has become famous, Godard features an actual interview with "Miss Nineteen." He prefaces the scene with the title, DIALOGUE WITH A CONSUMER PRODUCT. We prepare ourselves for an amusing satire on bourgeois vapidity, and we are not disappointed. "Miss Nineteen" is a pretty blonde who nervously toys with her hair. Suspicious of Paul's questions, she tries to avoid talking politics, but is drawn into a discussion of the differences between "the American way of life and the Socialist way." She loved America when she was there, particularly its fast pace and glamor. When Paul asks if she can think of a place where a war is taking place, she sidesteps the question prettily: "If I tried I could, but that doesn't interest me." After Paul asks her if she knows what "reactionary" means, the satiric balloon suddenly bursts, and we're left feeling a little less smug and superior. "Reactionary is being in opposition, reacting against things, not accepting just anything. I don't like yes-men." Though crudely stated, it is an anwer that could have been given by Paul—or Godard. But the *question* would have been different.

Near the end of the movie, Paul analyses the difficulties involved in searching for the truth, in arriving at wisdom. The scene begins with a shot that's strikingly similar to the one that opens the film. Paul sits at a café table, writing in his diary. The similarity of the shots suggests that he has come full circle: he's as much in the dark now as when he first began his investigation. Godard intercuts shots of crowds of people engaged in everyday activities, while we hear Paul's thoughts in a voice-over monologue:

Little by little during these three months, I've noticed that all these questions, far from reflecting a collective mentality, were frequently betraying and distorting it. My own lack of objectivity, often unconscious, most of the time corresponded to an inevitable lack of sincerity on the part of the people I was questioning . So, without knowing it, I was deceiving them and being deceived by them. Why? No doubt because polls and samples soon forget their true purpose, which is the observation of behavior, and insidiously substitute value judgments for research. I discovered that all the questions I was asking conveyed an ideolgy which didn't correspond to actual customs but to those of yesterday, of the past. Thus I had to remain vigilant. A few random observations came to me by chance and served me as guidelines. A philosopher is a man who pits his conscience against opinion: to have a conscience is to be open to the world. To be faithful is to act as if time did not exist. Wisdom would be if one could see life, really see, that would be wisdom.[9]

In many respects, the monologue could apply to Godard's search as well as Paul's. Both men recognize the dangers of "ideology," of excessive subjectivity, yet both realise that complete objectivity is impossible to achieve, and perhaps ultimately more dangerous. Paul's dilemma is finally resolved by his death: "He stepped back too far" and fell from a high window, Catherine tells the police in the final scene of the film. To paraphrase Godard, Paul's lack of subjectivity ultimately led him to a lack of objectivity.

There's a profound sense of frustration and failure throughout the film. Paul's unsuccessful search for clarity, for the Truth, is a reflection of Godard's own personal sense of frustration. This is best expressed in the scene where the youngsters go to the movies (fig. 14). The film they see is saturated with sexual sadism and masochism. While Madeleine, Elisabeth, and Catherine watch in fascination, Paul averts his eyes, and we hear his (and Godard's?) thoughts on the soundtrack:

This wasn't the film we'd dreamed of. This wasn't the total film that each of us had carried within himself . . . the film that we wanted to make, or, more secretly, no doubt . . . that we wanted to live. (p. 143)

---

9. This dialogue is quoted from the excellent transcription of the film which is edited by Pierre Billard and Robert Hughes (New York: Grove Press, Inc., 1969), pp. 174-177. The Billard-Hughes volume is a model of film scholarship and includes not only the action and dialogue, but over a hundred frame enlargements, most of them uncropped (although some are unfortunately reversed). All the shots are numbered, and the length of each is offered in parentheses. Also included are Maupassant's two stories, and a number of reviews of the film, both favorable and condemnatory. The translation of the dialogue is not always identical with that of the 16mm print which is distributed in the U.S., though discrepancies are minor. Subsequent dialogue quoted from this volume will be offered in parentheses in the text.

FIG. 14. *Masculine-Feminine*. The movie sequence. Even in a darkened theater Godard still used only available lighting. Throughout this scene, Paul and Elisabeth (Marlène Jobert) vie for Madeleine's attention. The man seated in the rear is totally "irrelevant" to the action.

Godard's identification with Paul is only partial, of course, though all too often, critics have assumed that the director and his characters are one. To equate Paul's ideological and personal failure with an *artistic* failure on Godard's part is to commit an absurdly simplistic blunder, for like Fellini's 8½, *(Otto e mezzo)* Godard's movie deals with the theme of failure with brilliant success.

Few contemporary directors can match Godard's extraordinary rapport with young adults. Kazan has captured the anguished solemnity of youth, Truffaut the charm and sweetness of the young, but Godard has gone beyond them, into contradictory, ambiguous realms that were only superficially explored before he arrived on the scene (fig. 15).

III

But Godard is more than the greatest chronicler of youth during the

FIG. 15. *Masculine-Feminine*. Godard's principal concern in this film was to reflect truly the lifestyles of the Parisian young, as in the strangely melancholy discothèque scene.

Sixties. He is also one of the world's most dazzling film technicians, an honor he shares with other directors, most notably Alain Resnais and Bernardo Bertolucci. Like Joyce with the novel, Godard has expanded and exploded the language of film, creating new forms and opening up an enormous range of technical possibilities for his successors. Like Joyce, Godard is a compulsive experimenter, plunging further and further toward the edge of incoherence. And as T.S. Eliot once said of Joyce, "it is the whole journey, not any stage of it, that assures him his place among the great."

In the area of sound alone, Godard has proved to be the most daring innovator since the experiments of Welles in the Forties. Like Welles, Godard feels that film shares many affinities with the theater, particularly in the use of language. His characters are good talkers, and their conversations range from pop culture to the most abstruse branches of philosophy. Indeed, Godard's discussions of his films are often couched in literary terms: "author," "essay," "novel," etc. Despite the fact that one of his recurrent themes is the failure of communication, his movies are luxuriant with language—spoken, printed, even sung.

Godard, however, uses language economically, and seldom merely to duplicate the information given by the visuals. He is fond of counterpointing monologues with non-synchronous visuals, as in one sequence where shots of workers, store windows, and streets are juxtaposed with the voice-over "thoughts" of the five young people: Paul contemplates the loneliness of the night; Madeleine prays for a car and TV, but asks to be "delivered" from freedom; Catherine muses on the transmitting of ideas by injection; Robert, on the effects of social existence on conscience; Elisabeth, on the stimulation of sexual pleasure through electronic devices.

Despite this profusion of words, one of Godard's principal themes is the impossibility of genuine personal communication, especially between the sexes. This is effectively dramatised in two parallel scenes. In the first, Paul records his declaration of love to Madeleine in a slot machine booth in an arcade. The scene is amusing, for his profuse outpouring is punctuated by a bizarre assortment of pop allusions. It is also sad by virtue of Paul's solitude: this is his most passionate declaration of love, yet it's delivered to a microphone, not to the loved one herself. Later in the movie, we see Madeleine during a recording session (fig. 16). Paul and Catherine wait while she intones the banal love lyrics of her song behind a soundproof window. Paul playfully tries to catch her attention, but Madeleine ignores him. Again, Godard stresses the isolating loneliness of love (Paul's) by keeping the two separated by the glass pane. From Madeleine's side of the window, we hear her frail tinny voice without musical accompaniment. Aurally, she's totally alone, yet the expression on her face betrays no sense of insufficiency. Paul's presence is merely an annoying irrelevance.

Godard's use of sound effects in this film is particularly bold. Indeed, his insistence upon natural sounds—all of them, as they were recorded on the set—dismays many critics, who complain of the "cacophonous din." But the noisy soundtrack is not due to artistic sloppiness, as some of his detractors claim. The movie deals with violence, the lack of privacy, and the lack of serenity. Simply by exploiting his soundtrack, Godard has no need to comment overtly on these themes—they're naggingly persistent in virtually every scene.

One of the most effective sound techniques is the use of gun shots for transitions. Often the abruptness of the editing is punctuated by the shattering blast of these shots, which have no visual source. Other scenes are accompanied by the cracking of billiard and bowling balls, the clattering of pinball machines, and the nervous stamping of a typewriter—all of them suggesting muffled gunfire shots. Important

FIG. 16. *Masculine-Feminine*. The recording session. Through the manipulation of sound and image, Godard simultaneously explores the themes of the debasement of culture and the pathos of solitude.

dialogue is sometimes drowned out by the noise of the street traffic, an adjoining conversation, or the clatter of dishes in a café. Because we are accustomed to a "clean" soundtrack—one from which all "extraneous" noises have been removed—we are unnerved by the noisiness of the movie. But of course, this is precisely Godard's point: he wishes to remind us that peace and serenity are absent in contemporary urban life.

Godard's use of music is seldom merely atmospheric, or employed as background filler. Often he makes "literary" comments of a broad or specific nature by juxtaposing music with a given scene. During the brief credit sequence, for example, we hear someone whistling a few bars of the French national anthem, suggesting that the following scenes are typical in some way of the whole nation. At one point in the movie, Paul clumsily asks Madeleine to marry him, a proprosal that meets with evasive annoyance. From a nearby jukebox, the lyrics of a tune reflect Madeleine's real sentiments: "I'm only your friend . . . Let me go my own way . . . " Paul is fond of Bach's Concerto in D and Mozart's Clarinet Concerto. This music represents for him a lost world of order, elegance and stability. The music and lyrics of Madeleine's songs are uniformly hackneyed and trifling—a perfect reflection, in fact, of her character. In an affectionate "homage" to a personal friend and colleague, Godard has Catherine sing a song from Truffaut's *Jules and Jim (Jules et Jim),* another allusion to a more stable and gracious era. Many commentators have criticised Godard (and Truffaut) for including "in-jokes" of this sort in their films. But Godard's allusions are not usually solely "homages." The lyrics of Catherine's song, for example, deal with the fickleness of women and how men are so easily deceived. In *Jules and Jim,* the song is sung by Jeanne Moreau, who also plays an ironic and jealous female named Catherine. For those familiar with Truffaut's film, the inclusion of this song in *Masculine-Feminine* is resonant with implications. The fact that the fascinating but bitchy heroine of Truffaut's movie literally kills her lover is not the least important of these implications.

One of the most striking techniques in *Masculine-Feminine* is the use of written titles between scenes, and sometimes even between shots of an interrupted scene. Generally, Godard uses these titles to speak directly to the audience—a form of Brechtian endistancing which helps the viewer to see a broader significance to a given scene or episode. Some titles are used to clarify the relationship of his parallel vignettes to the central characters. For example, in one scene, we see a blonde prostitute quarreling with two black men on a metro train. We see her secretly taking a gun from her purse. Suddenly the scene is concluded with four quick titles: NOTHING BUT A WOMAN/AND A MAN/ AND A SEA/ OF SPILLED BLOOD. Each of the titles is only two seconds in duration and is punctuated by the sound of a gun shot.

A number of titles are funny, and are included just for the hell of it. When the young people go to the movies, for example, the film they see is a parody of Ingmar Bergman's *The Silence (Tystnaden)*. Godard spoofs the image of the gloomy Swede by inserting the title: 4X: EIN SENSITIV UND RAPID FILM.[10] An interview scene between Robert and Catherine (fig. 17) ranges over a predictably wide gamut of subjects, including American movie stars, sex, and politics. After the scene ends, Godard wittily concludes: THIS FILM COULD BE CALLED/ THE CHILDREN OF MARX AND COCA COLA. There is an amusing instance of self-parody during the credit sequence,

---

10. Godard is punning. "4X" refers to a "fast" film stock which is highly sensitive to light. The "sensitive" qualities of the so-called "Swedish film" are a parody of the tender brutalities in *The Silence*. It is "rapid" because Paul leaves the theatre after a short time.

Godard's Masculine-Feminine: *The Cinematic Essay*

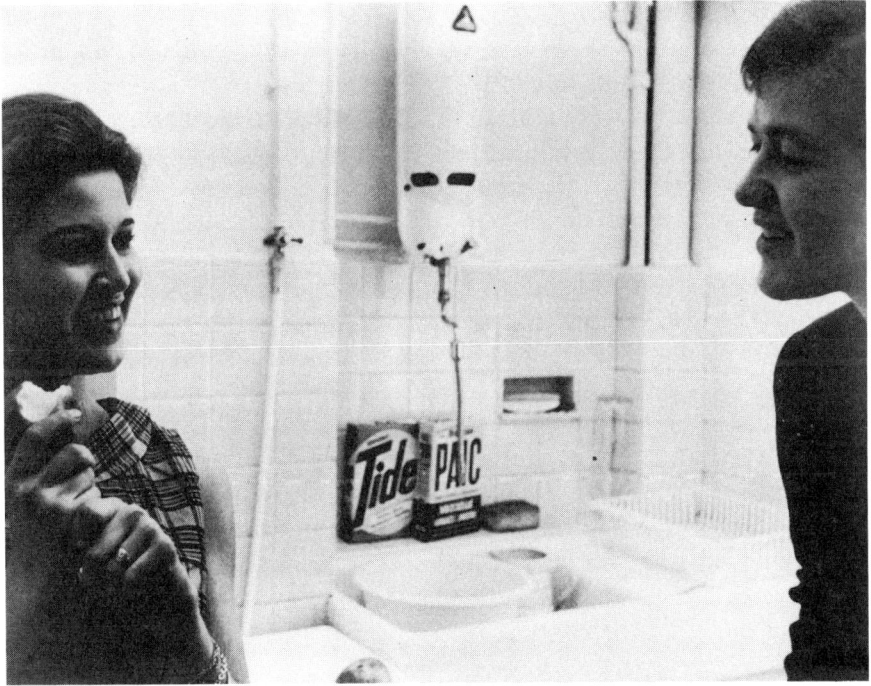

FIG. 17. *Masculine-Feminine*. Another lengthy interview scene, this one with the coy, temptress-like Catherine at one edge of the frame, and an eager Robert at the opposite corner. Brand names are featured throughout the film.

where Godard follows the film's title with: 15 PRECISE ACTS. Of course, there's nothing at all precise about the film's structure,[11] and to frustrate the viewer's expectations of neatness, Godard deliberately assigns arbitrary numbers to the episodes, and sometimes even skips the numbering of two or three scenes in a row. In one case, he satirises this desire for "precision" by introducing a scene with 4/A.

There are some critics who claim that the only major virtue in Godard's work is the photography, and that credit for the limited success of these films should go to Raoul Coutard, Godard's favorite cinematographer. True, Coutard is certainly one of the great cameramen presently working in the cinema, but *Masculine-Feminine*—photographically completely typical of Godard's work of this period—was shot by Willy Kurant. Coutard was cinematographer

---

11. In their transcription, Billard and Hughes (in one of their few lapses) seem to take Godard seriously. In a somewhat arbitrary manner, they attempt to assign a number to each of the major scenes in the film.

for Truffaut's *Shoot the Piano Player (Tirez sur le pianiste)*, *The Bride Wore Black (La mariée était en noir)*, the extravagantly lyrical *Jules and Jim* (fig. 18), and a number of other movies which bear little resemblance to the visual style of Godard's *oeuvre*.

In *Masculine-Feminine,* perhaps the most obvious characteristic of his visual style is in the lighting: there simply doesn't seem to be enough of it. Whole scenes are played in semi-darkened areas. And these are not the "artistically" stylised shadows of a glossy Hollywood movie, but actual dark spots created by the lack of additional lighting (figs. 14, 15). Godard uses "fast" stock, which permits him to shoot with available (i.e., natural) light, but when he sets his scenes in darkened interiors, we simply cannot see as clearly as we are accustomed. As is the case with his use of authentic sounds, the uneven shadows produced by available light are exploited primarily for symbolic reasons. Although the movie is set in the world's most beautiful city, the Paris of this film gasps for light, it's steeped in harsh shadows

FIG. 18. *Jules and Jim* (1961), directed by François Truffaut. Throughout the Sixties, Raoul Coutard was cinematographer on many of the films of Truffaut and Godard. Like most great cameramen, Coutard adjusted his visual style to suit the subject-matter—and the temperament of the directors.

and deep pools of blackness. The graininess of the images is a direct result of Godard's use of fast stock. But far from distracting from the effectiveness of the visuals, this graininess enhances a sense of documentary realism. There is a fortuitous quality to many of the images, almost as though a TV reporter happened upon them by chance.

The visuals of *Masculine-Feiminine* are not without beauty. Richard Roud has pointed out how Godard's images occasionally suggest a Vermeer painting.[12] Both artists display their light sources, often a window at one edge of the frame. Both reveal the exquisite beauty which can be discovered in perfectly ordinary objects when they are bathed by a certain kind of diffused lighting (fig. 2). The beauty of Godard's images is not found in a tourist's view of Paris, but rather in the sculptural contours of a face, a chair, or a cup, especially when they are softly caressed by the filtered lights of the late afternoon.

Throughout the film, Godard favors medium shots (fig. 19), though there are also a good number of close-ups. The reasons for this are not hard to determine. Long shots (which he avoids) are technically tricky, for many things can go wrong with them during filming—a dog might accidentally wander across the set, the actors might mistime their movements, etc. Godard dislikes having to shoot more than one or two takes, for he believes that a certain spontaneity and honesty are lost with repetition. By avoiding long shots, he also minimises the possibilities for anything going wrong, and hence, avoids the necessity of re-shooting. With medium shots, he can concentrate on one or two elements and control them more effectively. Since he also favors long takes, this control is all the more necessary, for he can then emphasise the nuances between two actors, the rhythms of a speech, or the psychological signficance of a little gesture or mannerism.

More important than these technical considerations is the fact that long shots are the most objective distances in film. The viewer is permitted to "sort out" the contents of the shot on his own, without becoming emotionally involved in the action. One of Godard's themes in this film concerns the twin dangers of subjectivity and objectivity. It's better to err on the side of excessive subjectivity than its opposite, he seems to imply. He acknowledges that close-ups are the most emotional (i.e., subjective) ranges in the cinema, and for this reason, he includes many of them, especially of Paul. The predominance of

---

12. See *Godard*, pp. 81-83. Roud offers a comparison between Vermeer's "Woman with Necklace" and a long shot from *Breathless*. A more Vermeer-like shot from *Masculine-Feminine* can be seen in the Billard-Hughes text on page 24.

FIG. 19. *Masculine-Feminine*. Throughout the film, Godard avoids shooting in depth, favors loosely framed medium shots, and avoids angles whenever possible.

medium shots, therefore, seems to be a kind of thematic compromise—a mid-point between the excessive objectivity of long shots and the distorting subjectivity of close-ups.

For similar reasons, Godard avoids angles. Virtually all the shots in the film are taken from eye level. From a strictly technical point of view, angles can be distressing: they often require correctional lighting, and the cranes that are sometimes necessary are expensive and cumbersome. Since Godard does not use studio sets, these problems are multiplied on location. But he avoids angles for "ethical" reasons as well. Almost inevitably, angles involve value judgments: by shooting down on a character, the director suggests a certain vulnerability, perhaps even a trace of authorial contempt. By shooting up towards the character, he is inevitably rendered heroic, awesome, or threatening. Godard does not patronise his characters with high angle shots, nor does he sentimentalise them with low angles. The eye-level camera approaches the characters as an equal, without prejudgements. It's objective, almost clinical. To be sure, Godard has opinions about his characters, but in general he avoids overt visual bias: he lets them reveal themselves. If he wishes to comment, he usually employs a conspicuous technique of authorial intrusion, like the insertion of written titles, which function in much the same way as the "Dear Reader" convention in Nineteenth century novels.

Godard's sense of "fair play" can also be seen in his avoidance of what might be called (for lack of a better term) the "anticipatory camera." Directors like Bergman or Welles tend to manipulate their actors so that their movements are anticipated by a stationary camera set-up: for the duration of the shot, the confines of the frame function much like the confines of the theatrical proscenium arch. In the movies of Bergman and Welles, this formal precision is often striking in its dance-like elegance and complexity. But thematically, Godard's later films stress freedom of choice, and the multiplicity of choices open to the characters. To use an anticipatory camera within this context is, in a way, to be at odds with the nature of the material. To avoid any sense of contrivance or predetermined action, Godard seems to place the camera at the disposal of his actors: it does not anticipate their movements, but dutifully follows the characters wherever they wish to lead. The placing of the camera seems rather tentative, there is a nervous quality about it, as though it could adjust easily to any alteration that might unexpectedly arise. Perhaps the most obvious instance of the anticipatory camera can be seen in scenes involving a running man. Most directors would place the camera on a direct line with the actor's path of motion. For example, if he runs from spot X to spot Z, one of the shots is likely to be taken from spot Z even *before* the actor gets there. Such a shot would show him running toward the camera. In some instances (in the movies of Lang or Hitchcock, for example), the camera might be "waiting" at spot Z even before the character himself knows where he'll turn. Most of Godard's later films avoid this type of set-up: it's too suggestive of predestination and fate. The "choice," in effect, has been determined in advance.

Even in shots involving no significant motion, Godard's camera seems prepared for several possible contingencies. This is especially true of the various café scenes, where the camera wanders off in a variety of directions, depending upon what catches the attention of the young people. Godard carries this principle of "preparedness" even to his framing (fig. 14). In one scene, for example, Paul and Elisabeth are eating dinner in a café, seated next to each other at a table. But instead of a two-shot, Godard includes a strange man at the same table in a three-shot. At first we are inclined to think he may be a friend, but the youngsters ignore him, and he sits quietly with almost equal indifference to them. Perhaps the young people will draw him in; perhaps he will speak to them. In either case, the camera is prepared. As it turns out, they never do acknowledge each other's presence: it's simply a matter of crowding at the tables. To some, the three-shot might seem to be a mere red herring, a typical instance of Godardian "perverseness." But there is more to the shot than this. It underlines the possibilities of choices open to the characters, and also dramatises the lack of privacy in the world of the film.

Another striking characteristic of Godard's visual style is the shallowness of his *mise-en-scè*ne. Unlike most directors, he deliberately flattens the depth of many of his images (fig. 20). Instead of the usual foreground-midground-background types of composition that most *metteurs-en-scène* strive to achieve, Godard simply places a character or group of characters along one visual plane, often with a flat backdrop to prevent the viewer's eye from wandering into the depth of the scene. He deliberately negates the third dimension of space, and the resultant effects have been compared to pop posters, comic strips, and mediaeval tapestries (fig. 21). Godard himself attributes the technique to Brecht's use of artificial theatrical tableaux.[13] The technique in-

FIG. 20. *La Chinoise* (1967), directed by Jean-Luc Godard. In his later works, Godard expanded many of the techniques found in *Masculine-Feminine,* particularly the avoidance of depth in favor of flat tableaux which are composed on only two visual planes.

13. See the Godard interview in *Interviews with Film Directors,* edited by Andrew Sarris (New York: Avon Books, 1967), p. 220.

FIG. 21. *Masculine-Feminine*. Godard once observed: "One might almost say that to live in society today is something like living inside an enormous comic strip."

volves certain advantages and liabilities. The most important loss is an absence of the complexity and richness that can be achieved by contrasting the various textures and spatial planes within the frame. For example, in *Ikiru*, Akira Kurosawa exploited the resources of deep-focus photography to compose his images on three, four, even five different planes (fig. 22). The complex psychological interrelationships that can be presented simultaneously through this technique are among the film's many triumphs, not to speak of the stunning visual richness.

But by flattening his images, Godard gains in technical ease, speed of execution, intensity of concentration, and symbolic suggestiveness. From a practical standpoint, he uses these methods because they are cheaper, faster, and simpler than using conventional techniques. Godard's small budgets force him to be resourceful, and resourcefulness in the cinema usually means shooting quickly, with a minimum of sets, props, costumes, lights, and re-takes. In some respects, a complex *mise-en-scène* can be likened to the technical complexity of long shots: they are difficult to achieve successfully because so many

FIG. 22. *Ikiru* (1952), directed by Akira Kurosawa. Godard attempts to make his images look "discovered" rather than "arranged." Kurosawa, on the other hand, composes his images with great precision, as in this deep-focus shot, which consists of at least five separate planes and is intricately balanced in its effect.

separate elements have to be harmonised simultaneously. If the action occurs in the midground, and something goes wrong in the foreground or background, the shot must be repeated until it's perfect. A method of avoiding these problems is simply to avoid depth in composition, an expedient traditionally employed in the old Hollywood B-films, which were made rapidly on very small budgets.

A good instance of Godard's resourcefulness in converting liabilities into advantages can be seen in the scene of the Vietnam protester's self-immolation. From a technical point of view, shooting the immolation would be expensive and time-consuming. Special precautions would have to be taken to insure the actor's safety. The scene would probably have to be photographed by several cameras simultaneously, to guarantee enough footage at the editor's bench. Very likely, retakes would be necessary. In all, an action taking less than a minute's screen time would require many hours to prepare and execute. Godard avoids all this by not shooting the immolation, but its *effects* on Paul and Catherine. To prevent the scene from appearing cheaply staged or contrived, Godard piques our curiosity through the humor of the matches gag. The entire scene is photographed before a blandly textured wall: our eyes are not permitted to wander, for there is no depth to the shot, and the camera is at medium range. We are forced to concentrate on the puzzled expressions of the actors. If Godard had shown the immolation, its effect would be intensely involving and shocking. By endistancing us from the main action, the scene actually becomes more complex, for it's simultaneously funny, grim, and intellectually provocative. By using these techniques, Godard is able to force the members of the audience to look where *he* wants them to. He is able to control their concentration with more precision—a valuable advantage for any didactic artist. Since Godard is one of the most technically resourceful of contemporary directors, this deliberate de-emphasis of spatial density is more than compensated for by the multitude of other techniques at his command.

The shallow *mise-en-scène* of the film is also thematically and symbolically appropriate. In a sense, the visual style is a perfect blend of "Marx and Coca Cola." Consumer goods, the Big Sell, capitalism — everywhere we look, we are reminded of Godard's political theme by the posters that plaster the walls. What could be more appropriate to a movie dealing with pop culture and pop politics than a visual style that suggests a pop poster? "One might almost say that to live in society today is something like living inside an enormous comic strip," Godard has remarked.[14] In his subsequent films, especially *La Chinoise*, he was to employ this poster-comic strip style with even greater effect (figs. 23, 24).

The editing style in *Masculine-Feminine* is as brilliant as it was in *Breathless*, when he virtually revolutionised montage practices, and, along with Truffaut and Resnais, set the pace for most of the best films of the following decade. Precisely because Godard has helped to overturn traditional patterns of editing, we are perhaps inclined to take his bold experiments for granted. The "look" of the films of the Sixties is due in large part to his trail-blazing: the shifts in rhythm mid-scene, the unmatched shots, the abrupt tone breaks, the disorienting jump-cuts, the lack of transitional bridging shots, the incredibly long takes—these and more are directly traceable to Godard's practices in his early films. In *Masculine-Feminine*, there are many shots that last a fraction of a second. The "Miss Nineteen" interview, on the other hand, is almost seven minutes in length, and is photgraphed in one

---

14. Godard himself makes this statement in his movie, *Two or Three Things I Know about Her* (*Deux ou trois choses que je sais d'elle*, 1966).

FIG. 23. *La Chinoise*. In his later works, Godard expanded his tableau technique to include drawings, printing, live actors, and symbolic props.

FIG. 24. *Blood of a Poet* (1929), directed by Jean Cocteau. Godard has always been an enthusiastic champion of the films of Cocteau, who has been called the Father of the New Wave. Cocteau's stylistic eclecticism— especially in his Orpheus films—was an obvious influence on Godard's later works.

Godard's Masculine-Feminine: *The Cinematic Essay* 55

uninterrupted take. Few film-makers apart from Godard would be bold enough to attempt such a shot, yet it's brilliantly successful, in large part because of his refusal to edit the footage in order to make it fit a convenient thesis.

Godard delights in breaking the "rules" of film-making, all the old saws about how certain scenes and sequences "should" be shot. His detractors pounce upon him for his "self-indulgent rebelliousness," often forgetting that today's innovations have a way of becoming tomorrow's conventions. In fact, many of Godard's "innovations" are not at all new. Precedents can be found for many of his techniques, and Godard is perfectly aware of his predecessors: indeed, many of his most outlandish scenes are deliberate "homages" to past (and often neglected) masters of the film (figs. 25, 26). In a laundromat scene in the movie, for example, Paul tells Robert a shaggy dog story, and the sequence is edited in a series of unmatched shots: the soundtrack is continuous (Paul's narration), but the visuals are disconnected, showing Paul at various stages in laundering his clothes. As far back as the

FIG. 25. *Scarface* (1932), directed by Howard Hawks. Visual and verbal "homages" to the *genre* films of Hawks, Lang, and Fuller are common in the early works of Godard.

FIG. 26. *La Chinoise*. Even in Godard's later films, the influence of these American *genre* masters can often be discerned, though the homages are characteristically transformed to suit Godard's own symbolic purposes.

early Thirties, when sound techniques were being explored, Ernst Lubitsch and René Clair used similar techniques. Vincente Minnelli (another Godard favorite) employed this technique extensively in the musical numbers of *Gigi*. Today, unmatched visuals with a continuous soundtrack are employed even in routine TV commercials.

Godard's handling of actors is also unorthodox. He has been criticised for being a poor director of performers, and this is certainly true of a number of his films, particulary those which feature his ex-wife, Anna Karina. But he has also used some excellent performers, like Jean-Paul Belmondo and Jean-Pierre Léaud, the latter playing Paul in *Masculine-Feminine*. Godard has stated that in most instances, he uses a specific actor not for his gifts of impersonation, but for what he *is*: in other words, typecasting, a much-maligned, but perfectly respectable practice, cheerfully admitted to by such diverse directors as Eisenstein, Hitchcock, and Rossellini (fig. 27). In *Contempt,* for example, Godard used Brigitte Bardot and Jack Palance virtually to play themselves. Palance, a performer of considerable range, was irritated with Godard because he would not give the actor any assistance in

FIG. 27. *Paisan* (1946), directed by Roberto Rossellini. Godard was strongly influenced by Rossellini's use of non-professional actors, even for major roles. Perhaps Godard's most Rossellinian film is *Les carabiniers* (1963), on which the Italian director served as one of the writers.

interpreting his "character." But Palance—and some critics as well—rather missed the point. As Godard has explained, Palance "didn't have to act, just the fact of his being there was already a kind of performance."[15]

In *Masculine-Feminine* too, the "acting" (with the exception of Léaud's) can hardly qualify for that term. For the most part, the performers seem to play themselves. Chantal Goya, who plays Madeleine, is actually a pop singer who had never acted in a movie before. As is the case in many of Godard's films, the young people were encouraged to improvise much of their dialogue, or were simply given a general notion of what to say. What Godard wanted from them above all was "authenticity." According to him, the role of the director in relationship to the actors is like an interviewer with a person interviewed. Even the acting, then, is a kind of investigation, a process of discovery:

15. Quoted in "Excerpt from an Interview with Richard Grenier and Jean-Luc Godard," by James Blue, in Mussman, *op cit.*, p. 250.

I like to sneak up on an actor from behind, leaving him to fend for himself, following his groping movements in the part, trying to seize on the sudden, unexpected, good moment which crops up spontaneously.[16]

IV

Masculine-Feminine is the cinematic counterpart to Montaigne's familiar essay in almost every respect. Neither artist worked from a preconceived plan. The "attempts" of both are exploratory, not definitive. Godard's movie does not pretend to be an exhaustive analysis of the Nature of Youth, but a personal, tentative investigation of some Parisian youngsters at a certain point in history. The director suggests that his qualified conclusion is subject to even further qualification in subsequent works. Both essayists demonstrate a considerable humility before the evidence. They dislike dogmatism and prefer to reserve final judgment.

Like Montaigne's essays, *Masculine-Feminine* is intensely self-conscious. We are always aware of the author's personality—of his likes and dislikes, his values, even his anxieties. But the conspicuous presence of the artist's personality is no mere ego-tripping. Like many "confessional" authors, Godard, like Montaigne, presents us with a self-portrait in order that we may gain insights into "human nature" in general. Both authors, in short, are ultimately concerned with universals. In each case, the view of human nature is skeptical and playfully ironic, yet not without a certain underlying idealism and hope. Both men view the human condition as contradictory and paradoxical (fig. 28). Changeability and ambivalence are the basic human traits, they seem to believe.

Both Montaigne and Godard are stylistically eclectic: they mix fictional and "documentary" elements, personal digressions, autobiography, quotations from other sources, and a great deal of ironic humor to explore their subjects. Both are willing to hazard any technique that might help their audiences to understand the complex, contradictory nature of their topics. Godard has been criticised for his eclecticism, for trying "to cover the whole ground, from all possible angles, saying everything at once," to use his own self-mocking description. But at his best—and *Masculine-Feminine* represents his best—Godard could be described in the same terms that Ralph Waldo Emerson used in summing up the achievement of Montaigne:

---

16. Quoted in Milne, *op. cit.*, p. 85.

Godard's Masculine-Feminine: *The Cinematic Essay* 59

FIG. 28. *Weekend*. One of Godard's harshest indictments of contemporary capitalist societies, *Weekend* is characteristically ambivalent, for the hippie-revolutionaries behave almost as savagely as the members of the society that they are trying to displace.

There have been men with deeper insight; but, one would say, never a man with such abundance of thoughts: he is never dull, never insincere, and has the genius to make the reader care for all that he cares for.

2
The Aesthetic of the Mobile Camera

The dolly shot is a moral statement.
—Jean-Luc Godard

Even in the most prosaically utilitarian contexts, the mobile camera can suggest certain symbolic ideas. (Throughout my dicussion, I will use the term "mobile camera" in the generic sense, to include all vehicular—dolly and crane—movements, and those zoom shots that are obviously meant to suggest the camera moving through space.) In general, however, the symbolism of the mobile camera arises from the literalness and function of the shot.

For example, Buster Keaton's *Cops* opens with a medium shot of Buster behind bars. We naturally assume that he has been arrested and imprisoned. But when the camera dollys back to a long shot distance, we realise that he is simply standing behind a large iron gate of a garden, talking to his girl-friend. On the most obvious level, the shot is a mild joke at the audience's expense. But the shot functions on a symbolic level as well. Keaton's comedy is based on the idea of a conflict between Buster and certain "hostile" objects within a given space (fig. 1). These objects can be machines, guns, a locomotive — anything that the hero views with suspicion or anxiety. We generally find the idea of a *man* fighting for dominance over a *thing* an amusing spectacle. That these things *do* seem hostile only intensifies our

FIG. 1. *The General* (1926), directed by Buster Keaton and Clyde Bruckman. At the conclusion of this film, Johnnie Gray (Keaton) is commissioned an officer. He withdraws with girl for some quiet romancing, but various passing soldiers interrupt the lovers, for Johnnie is now required to salute every soldier. With some readjusting in space, however, our hero manages to kiss his girl and salute his troops at the same time.

amusement. In Keaton's movies, the frame functions as a metaphor for Buster's "field" of concentration (fig. 2). That is, anything outside the frame is irrelevant to the struggle which will ensue. But in the shot from *Cops,* the space is sneakily redefined by the mobile camera.

Essentially, this is also the philosophical dimension of Keaton's comedy. No one can approach, apprise, and master objects in space with quite the same aplomb as Buster when he is determined to be master. But often—through luck or Fate—the object alters in some way, it refuses to remain passive, to "co-operate" with his desires. Hence the comedy. Objects—like life itself— are never permanent: no sooner does Buster seem to be on top of things (sometimes literally) than everything suddenly changes, and the victory turns out to be a Pyrrhic one. The dolly-back in Keaton's opening shot is the director's ironic joke on the audience, giving us a small dose of what it feels like to be "tricked" by an unpredictable alteration of circumstances. The symbolism of the mobile camera in this shot suggests the perverse

FIG. 2. *The Navigator* (1924), directed by Buster Keaton and Donald Crisp. Keaton's spatial comedy is usually dependent upon his expert use of the frame. In this shot, the camera is close enough to photograph the necessary details (the tiny egg, the watch, Keaton's solemn face), yet just far enough away to include comic contrasts (the huge kettle he plans to use to boil the egg.)

whimsies of Fate. It also implies abstract ideas of flux and impermanence, characteristic elements of many dolly shots.

As in most of Keaton's best films, form follows function, and symbolic meaning is an extension of the literal. It's perfectly possible to understand Keaton's gag and not even notice its symbolic implications. There have always been other film-makers who have used traveling shots less "functionally"—Max Ophüls comes immediately to mind. Within the past decade, however, the use of the mobile camera for *primarily* symbolic or metaphoric purposes has become more common.

But first, function. In the days when elaborate tracks had to be laid for dolly shots (hence the term "tracking shot"), a director was generally held strictly accountable by his studio, for such shots were both complex and very expensive (figs. 3, 4). In effect, the mobile camera

FIG. 3. The use of the mobile camera usually involves elaborate preparations and expense. Note the additional lighting and the lengthy tracks necessary for this moving shot for example. The camera (at right, under the umbrella) will dolly from the right to the extreme left in one continuous movement.

FIG. 4. When the floor is even, as in this studio set, long boards are often used instead of tracks for a traveling shot. In some instances, the boards are whisked in or out of place while the camera is actually in motion, for otherwise the boards would be included in the final image.

removed the edges of the frame: the lighting technicians were responsible not only for the enclosed area within the frame, but also for those "outside" areas which the camera would traverse in a continuous movement. Similarly, sets had to be more elaborate, since they had to continue for as long and far as the shot traveled. The *mise-en-scène* was necessarily more complex: the film-maker was responsible not only for the arrangements and movements of volumes within the

FIG. 5. On the set of *Letter from an Unknown Woman* (1948), directed by Max Ophüls. Before the perfection of the hand-held camera, elaborate cranes had to be used in order to photograph a character walking up a winding staircase. In shots such as these, Ophüls was required virtually to choreograph the movements of the camera with the actors. Needless to say, his producers would have preferred stationary set-ups, with a number of different shots edited together to give the *illusion* of a continuous movement.

The Aesthetic of the Mobile Camera

spatial planes of a single frame, but throughout the varying depths and textures of the elongated set (fig. 5). Dolly shots are time-consuming, both in preparation and in terms of screen time. They can slow the pace of a movie unless a director uses them only at strategically right moments. With the wide-spread practice of location shooting and the improved equipment of today's film-makers, these problems are less acute, but traveling shots are still generally more complex to set up than those employing a stationary camera (fig. 6).

One of the major advantages of the mobile camera is in its preservation of the continuity of space and time. The moving camera in many instances is a more logical alternative to montage, for the art of editing tends to be based on an aesthetic of fragmentation. André Bazin formulated a principle concerning these differences: "When the essence of a scene demands the simultaneous presence of two or more factors in the action, montage is ruled out."[1] In our context, Bazin's

FIG. 6. Even on location, with a minimum of interference, dolly shots are still generally more complicated than most stationary set-ups.

---

1. "The Virtues and Limitations of Montage, from *What is Cinema?* (Berkeley: University of California Press, 1967), p. 50.

"law" means that the mobile camera is a more effective way of connecting two or more integrally-related elements than the splicing of separate shots, which tends to isolate the elements (fig. 7).

FIG. 7. *North by Northwest* (1959), directed by Alfred Hitchcock. The famous crop-dusting plane sequence from this film is a good illustration of Bazin's principle. If Hitchcock had cut from separate shots of the plane to shots of the running protagonist (Cary Grant), the terrifying power of the sequence would probably be lost, for we would not know the exact spatial relationship between these two elements.

The Aesthetic of the Mobile Camera

John Huston's *The African Queen* contains a shot which clarifies Bazin's principle. In attempting to take their boat down river to a large lake, the two protagonists (Humphrey Bogart and Katharine Hepburn) get sidetracked on a tributary of the main river. The tributary dwindles into a stream, and finally trickles into a tangle of reeds and mud, where the dilapidated boat gets hopelessly mired (fig. 8.). The exhausted travelers resign themselves to a slow death in the suffocating reeds, and eventually fall asleep on the floor of the boat. The camera then moves upward, over the reeds, and there—just a few hundered yards away—is the lake. The bitter irony of the scene is conveyed by the continuous movement of the camera, which preserves the proximity of the boat, the intervening reeds, and the lake. If Huston had cut to three separate shots, we would not understand these spatial inter-rclationships, and hence, the irony would be sacrificed.

FIG. 8. *The African Queen* (1952), directed by John Huston. Throughout this film Huston avoided cutting between shots of his actors and shots of the locale. Whenever possible, he used pans, tilts, crane and dolly shots to emphasise the physical connection between the protagonists and the setting.

In *You Only Live Once,* Fritz Lang used several traveling shots to convey his theme of philosophical determinism. He succeeds precisely because of the viewer's tendency to accept the "connectedness" of objects that are photographed in one continuous movement. The movie begins with a close-up of some apples on a desk. We see a hand take one of the apples and assume that it's being pilfered. When the camera dollys back, however, we realize that a fruit peddler is merely demonstrating how his fruit is constantly being stolen by the police officer on his beat. Despite its ominous beginning, the scene is treated in an essentially comic manner.

Later in the film, Lang repeats this technique. Eddie Taylor (Henry Fonda), the ex-con protatgonist of the movie, has been fired from his job, and is in desperate need of cash. A sequence in a dingy hotel room begins with a close-up of Taylor's hat, which has his initials inside the brim. The camera then travels (still in close-up range) to other objects in the room, resting finally on a close-up of a revolver. The audience assumes—again mistakenly—that Eddie has returned to a life of crime.

Somewhat later, in a brilliantly executed bank robbery sequence, Lang employs this *motif* a third time. (Ironically, Eddie is referred to as a "three-time loser" in the film). Inside the robber's car, we see another close-up of Eddie's initialed hat. The camera then moves to include guns, gas bombs, and gas masks, which the thieves put on just before they strike. We never actually see the faces of the bank robbers, but naturally assume that Eddie is one of them—an assumption also shared by the police later in the film when they find Eddie's hat on the scene of the crime. Eventually we learn that we were wrong again. The hat was planted on the scene by Eddie's former cell-mate in a spiteful act of revenge. By keeping his camera at close-up range and then "connecting" certain objects through the use of the three traveling shots, Lang—somewhat like Keaton—is able to show the dangers of association and "logic." In this film, we are as guilty as the police, for like them, we have assented to a facile assumption of guilt by circumstantial evidence. What Lang unfolds so powerfully in the film is how isolated "evidence"—the close-ups—are merely single strands of an elaborate web of Destiny: a web that ultimately succeeds in ensnaring its victim.

Lang's dolly shots are used to connect objects in a unified space, but traveling shots can also be used to preserve the temporal continuity of a scene. Particularly in suspenseful sequences, the dolly shot tends to elongate time, and hence draw out the suspense. In Hitchcock's *Psycho,* for example, the heroine (Vera Miles) searches in the rooms of a darkened house, while her accomplice tries to detain the suspicious owner in a motel office just outside the house. Working against

The Aesthetic of the Mobile Camera

time, the girl searches from room to room, while the camera follows her, prolonging the agony for both the heroine and the audience. In Bazin's terms, the essence of the scene is in the expiration of a limited amount of *time* in relationship to the vastness of the house. The suspenseful juxtapostion of these two elements is intensified by Hitchcock's use of the time-consuming dolly shots.

An additional principle can be deduced from this example. If the *experience* of movement rather than its goal or destination is the purpose of a shot, it's better to dolly than to cut. In other words, if a director wishes to emphasise a woman's anxiety in moving from place to place, he is more likely to dolly after her, or use the point-of-view-dolly, which would simulate her movements. But if the director is more concerned with *what* she'll find than with the process of finding it, he's more likely to cut, in order to eliminate unnecessary time and space between the inception of the movement and its conclusion.

The mobile camera is often used as an establishing device. Generally, the director provides an extreme long shot of a locale to provide the context of a scene, then moves in for a closer view of where the action will occur (fig. 9). To take another example from *Psycho*, the film opens with an extreme long shot of the skyline in Phoenix, Arizona. While the camera slowly moves in, the image dissolves to a tall hotel building in Phoenix. With the camera still moving closer, we finally arrive at a specific window of the hotel, where two illicit lovers are having a rendezvous. The moving camera in this instance is not only an establishing device, but a symbolic *motif* which is repeated several times in the film, suggesting a kind of voyeurism, a probing into the intimate lives and personalities of others.

The pull-back dolly is a way of revealing previously withheld information, and often it is used to establish an important detail before moving back to explore its larger implications (fig. 10). In Truffaut's *The Wild Child (L'enfant sauvage)* for instance, we see a hunting party with a pack of hounds pursuing a terrified twelve-year-old child through the wilderness. The naked boy is covered with filth and weeds—more animal than human. In desperation, the creature scrambles up a tall tree to hide. Truffaut shows us a close-up of his face: panic-stricken, exhausted, his eyes darting furtively from side to side. Then the camera begins to zoom out slowly, and as it does, the boy is swallowed up by the dense foliage of the tree. The zoom stops at an extreme long shot and the boy is now a microscopic speck on the screen. In effect, the backward movement embodies eight years of history, for we later learn that the child was abandoned at the age of four, and miraculously survived, growing up virtually as an animal in the forest.

FIG. 9. *Intolerance* (1916), directed by D. W. Griffith. In the Babylonian sequence of his epic masterpiece, Griffith used an incredibly elaborate "crane" shot (actually, tracks were used), which photographed the enormous set from hundreds of yards away, then swooped down to within a few feet of some of the revellers below.

FIG. 10. *A Clockwork Orange* (1972), directed by Stanley Kubrick. The film opens with an extreme close-up of Alex (Malcolm McDowell), which helps to establish his point of view in the narration. Kubrick then dollys back to reveal the protagonist's surroundings.

A common function of the mobile camera is to provide an ironic contrast with dialogue. In Jack Clayton's *The Pumpkin Eater,* for example, a distraught wife (Anne Bancroft) returns to an ex-husband's house where she has an adulterous liaison with him. As the two lie in bed, she asks him if he had been upset over their divorce, and whether or not he missed her. He assures her that he wasn't in the least upset, but while his voice continues on the soundtrack, the camera belies his words by slowly dollying through his living room, revealing pictures, memorabilia, and mementos of the ex-wife. The shot is a direct communication between the director and the audience. In a sense, shots of this sort can be compared with an omniscient narrator in a novel providing the reader with information which the characters lack. These techniques are deliberate authorial intrusions, and are particularly favored by film-makers who view their characters with skepticism or irony—Godard, Hitchcock, and Lubitsch, for example.

Sometimes the mobile camera is used to communicate psychological rather than physical revelations. By dollying in on a character, the director can suggest that character's emotional response to a given situation. In Arthur Penn's *Alice's Restaurant,* for example, the heroine (Pat Quinn) has been assured by her immature husband that he will change his ways and become more stable and responsible . In a later scene, he rambles drunkenly to a group of friends about his plans for the future, plans that are childishly unrealistic. During the scene, the camera dollys in on the wife's face, slowly revealing her realisation that her husband hasn't changed at all (fig. 11). Dolly shots of this kind emphasise a character's gradual comprehension of a situation. The camera's arrival at its destination (the close-up) is, in effect, a metaphor for the character's "arrival" at complete realisation.

The distinction between a predominantly functional and symbolic dolly shot is not always an easy one to make, as can be seen from the example from *Alice's Restaurant*. Many of the illustrations offered above suggest symbolic ideas, but they are primarily functional in purpose. That is, the shots were dictated by certain problems involving time and space—problems which could be best solved through the use of the mobile camera. The following examples will concentrate on predominantly metaphoric uses of the moving camera, though in some cases these shots serve perfectly functional purposes as well.

By exploiting an audience's kinetic responses, a director can employ certain camera movements to convey a character's internalised emotions. In some respects, shots of this sort suggest that the camera is a dancer, expressing ideas and feelings through pure movement. Most viewers associate given movements with symbolic meanings. An upward motion, for example, tends to suggest freedom, exultation, joy.

FIG. 11. *Alice's Restaurant* (1969), directed by Arthur Penn. One of the most common uses of the mobile camera is to emphasise a character's slow comprehension of a given situation. Such dolly shots also tend to reinforce that character's isolation from his surroundings.

In Truffaut's *Jules and Jim,* the lilting upward sweep of a helicopter shot is used to convey Jim's exhilaration when he plans to visit his friend Jules after a lengthy separation. Literally, the shot doesn't make much sense: it's not even historically accurate, for the period of the sequence is about 1918 (fig.12). The shot functions on another level entirely; it is used as a metaphor of Jim's sense of release and transcendent joy.

Downward motions, on the other hand, tend to suggest heaviness, exhaustion, and defeat. In *The Pawnbroker,* Sidney Lumet used an elaborate crane shot to convey a number of these ideas. An aging self-centered pawnbroker (Rod Steiger) has deliberately withdrawn from all human contact throughout the film. He is often photographed from behind the wire cages of his shop, suggesting a kind of self-imposed imprisonment—a barricaded cell where people cannot reach him, either physically or emotionally (fig. 13). Late in the film, three thugs invade his shop and attempt to rob him. The pawnbroker's

FIG. 12. *Jules and Jim* (1961), directed by François Truffaut. The New Wave French directors popularised the use of the lightweight hand-held camera for certain scenes. In Truffant's movie, for example, cinematographer Raoul Coutard photographed a bicycling sequence while riding a bike himself. The graceful swirling movements of these shots would have been impossible to capture with traditional methods of shooting.

FIG. 13. *The Pawnbroker* (1965), directed by Sidney Lumet. Throughout the film, the protagonist imprisons himself behind the wire cages of his pawnshop. In the climactic scene, Lumet shows the liberating of the pawnbroker's spirit through the use of a spectacular crane shot, in which the camera climbs the steep walls of the wire cages to the outside world of freedom and responsibility.

youthful assistant tries to stop the thugs from killing the old man after he refuses to open his safe. As the youth advances, he is shot by one of the thieves. Writhing in agony on the floor, the boy crawls painfully from the shop to the crowded street outside. Lumet photographs this scene from behind the pawnbroker's wire cage, in what appears to be a point-of-view shot. With the discordant music intensifying to an anguished shriek, the camera cranes up, over the high wire cage. This upward surge conveys the joyous emotional release the old man feels when he realises that the impulsive youngster has risked his life to save his employer. But the exhilaration is only momentary, for the camera then plunges down the other side of the cage in a swooping motion that is meant to suggest the pawnbroker's sudden realisation that his assistant is fatally wounded.

More complex (and rare) are pendular movements of the camera which can suggest monotony and boredom. In Godard's *La Chinoise*, some youthful Maoists are shown in their communal appartment engaging in an ideological dispute. One group sits at one end of the room, the other at the opposite end. Instead of cutting from one group to the other with their dialogue, Godard dollys back and forth for the duration of the scene, a conspicuous and apparently clumsy technique. From a strictly functional point of view, Godard's method of filming the scene is clearly not the most efficient approach, but in this case, function follows form (fig. 14). The pendular movements of the camera convey metaphorically the monotonous but necessary refinement of ideas of the dialectical process. Like the shot itself, this dialectical refinement seems cumbersome and tedious, particularly to an outsider. Despite its apparent crudity, Godard's shot is organically fused with his subject-matter: each swing of the camera represents a thesis or antithesis. The end result, presumably, will be a synthesis of opposites.

Circular movements of the camera have occasionally been used metaphorically, though not always with such freshness and subtlety. In *Love Story*, for example, the camera performs a 360° turn around the two lovers during the wedding ceremony: the circular movement is meant to symbolise the marriage ring. In *The Manchurian Candidate*, John Frankenheimer used a circular movement with more daring and wit during several dream sequences. Some American prisoners of the Korean War have been brainwashed, and are being exhibited to a group of Communist observers in a laboratory amphitheater. During the sequences, we also see what the brainwashed soldiers *think* is going on: that they are temporarily detained in a New Jersey hotel, listening to a lecture on horticulture which is being presented to a group of genteel dowagers. Several times, Frankenheimer circles the entire assembly by beginning with the speaker's platform, scanning the

The Aesthetic of the Mobile Camera

FIG. 14. *Breathless* (1959), directed by Jean-Luc Godard. In his first feature, Godard wanted many dolly shots, but his modest budget forbade the use of elaborate equipment. Ever the improviser, Godard strapped his cameraman in a wheelchair while the director himself propelled Coutard in the direction of the action.

audience, then circling back to the other end of the platform. Throughout these shots, two "realities" merge: genteel ladies are incongruously linked with Communist observers. The dreamers (who are still partially brainwashed many months later) are unable to make sense of these weird mixtures of settings, characters, and events. Frankenheimer uses the circular *motif* as a metaphor of psychological determinism, a programmed pattern that begins to "short circuit" after the prisoners are released and sent back to America. The metaphor of circuitry is used several times in the dialogue as well ("The wires have been pulled, Raymond—you're free").

In his later films, Federico Fellini has experimented widely with the symbolic implications of dolly shots. In *8½* in particular, he employs them as a thematic *motif*. Guido, the protagonist (Marcello Mastroianni) is a film director who is trying to put together a movie near a bizarre health spa. Everywhere he turns, he is confronted by memories, fantasies, and "realities" more fantastic than anything he can imagine; but he is paralysed by indecision: what (if anything) from all this copious flux and superabundance will he select for his movie? He cannot use everything, since it would not cohere—the materials are too sprawling. Throughout the film, the camera wanders restlessly, prowling over the fantastic locale, compulsively hoarding images of faces, textures, and shapes. All are absorbed by Guido, but he is unable to detach them from their contexts to form a meaningful artistic structure. The film's traveling shots function on several levels. They are used to suggest Guido's increasingly desperate search for a theme, a story, or a cinematic structure. They are also analogues of Guido's passive receptivity: he is a walking recording machine, seeking out and storing image upon image for their own sake. The traveling shots, in conjunction with the movement of people, processions, and traffic, are also analogues for the unbroken flow of experiences which comprises Guido's reality, a reality he ultimately refuses to simplify for the sake of producing a tidy packaged movie. But where Guido fails, Fellini succeeds triumphantly. The final sequence of the film (which takes place in Guido's imagination) emphasizes the continuity and coherence of his experiences. The characters from the film—including those of Guido's past and fantasies—join hands and dance joyously around a circus ring. The ring is a perfect visual symbol of Fellini's conception of life's infinite flow, a flow that has no beginning or end.

Camera movements inevitably alter the composition of a shot. Generally speaking, a dolly-in tends to tighten the frame and its action while a dolly-out loosens the composition. In *The Wild Bunch,* Sam Peckinpah used two slight zoom shots as metaphors of psychological tension and release. The wild bunch are bringing in a wagonload of weapons and munitions when they are ambushed by Mexican soldiers. Rather than give up the load to the soldiers, the bunch threaten to blow it up—and themselves with it. The decision rests with the Mexican officer. As he quickly sizes up the situation, the camera zooms in to a closer position, framing the officer in a tighter composition. Realising that he has been outwitted, the officer smiles ironically, and agrees to let the bunch pass with the wagon. As he does so, the camera zooms back to its former position, thus releasing the tensions of the tight frame. The shot functions almost like a screw, which turns in on the officer while he's under pressure to make a quick decision, then loosens after he decides.

Many symbols and metaphors are derived from the very physical properties of the mobile camera: abstract ideas involving space, time, energy, and penetration. Since the camera literally travels, directors have often used its movement as a metaphor for a journey of some kind. In *Paths of Glory,* for example, Stanley Kubrick expanded the

The Aesthetic of the Mobile Camera

metaphor of the title with several spectacular dolly shots satirising military stupidities. The setting is the First World War, in the trenches of the front line (fig.15). Some French soldiers have been ordered to take over an impregnable German hill fortification by an ambitious general. Both the general and the conscripted men realise it's a hopeless mission, that most of them will die in the attempt. On the day that the troops are to leave their trenches, the general comes to wish them luck. In an incredibly smooth and lengthy dolly shot, the camera sweeps efficiently through the narrow winding trenches, as the General whisks past his troops, patronising them with bad jokes and fatuous predictions of success. The smooth elegant dollying through the trenches represents the general's real "path" of glory—safely behind the front lines.

The camera then leaves the trenches with the soldiers, as they venture on the raging battlefield. The camera doggedly stays with the soldiers, as they zigzag around explosions, inch ahead slightly, then retreat, then go forward again. All the while, soldiers are dropping

FIG. 15. *Paths of Glory* (1957), directed by Stanley Kubrick. In keeping with the metaphor of the film's title, Kubrick employed some of the most famous traveling shots in cinematic history in this film. The director admitted to the influence of Max Ophüls.

everywhere, and the roar of the guns is stupefying. The troops are decimated as they bravely—and absurdly—push forward. Only a few tattered men are left alive. They decide to turn back, and with their retreat, the camera turns back too, as they crawl to the protection of the trenches. This futile "path" of glory turns out to be as hollow and meaningless as the first.

The mobile camera can suggest the temporal aspects of a journey as well. For example, Sidney Lumet used a traveling shot for his central metaphor in his adaptation of Eugene O'Neill's *Long Day's Journey into Night*. The "journey" of the title is itself a metaphor for an examination of the past, and how it determined the present for the doomed Tyrone family. The "night" symbolises Mary Tyrone's tragic addiction to morphine, and the grief it causes to the other members of the family. Near the end of the the film, James Tyrone and his two sons sit at a table, almost immobilised by whiskey. Mary—by now totally immersed in drugs—comes downstairs, and rambles about her experiences when she was a young girl in the convent school and wanted to be a nun. As she does, the camera cranes back from a medium position to a long, to an extreme long shot range: the entire family shrinks to a small speck of light on the screen, surrounded by a vast *matte* of blackness. The camera's slow movement backward suggests Mary's drug-induced return to the past—the "journey" of the title.

A number of directors have exploited the mobile camera as a *consumer* of time, most notably Orson Welles (especially in *The Magnificent Ambersons*) and Alain Resnais, whose major films center around the theme of time. The acknowledged master of these types of dolly shots is Max Ophüls, about whom James Mason wrote a charming poem:

> I think I know the reason why
> Producers tend to make him cry.
> Inevitably they demand
> Some stationary set-ups , and
> A shot that does not call for tracks
> Is agony for poor dear Max,
> Who, separated from his dolly,
> Is wrapped in deepest melancholy.
> Once, when they took away his crane,
> I thought he'd never smile again.[2]

---

2. Quoted as a headnote in *Interviews with Film Directors,* edited by Andrew Sarris (New York: Avon Books, 1969), p. 350.

The Aesthetic of the Mobile Camera

As Andrew Sarris points out in his perceptive discussion of the director, Ophüls uses dolly shots as metaphors of time's cruel prodigality (figs. 16, 17, 18). His world is one of tragic flux and mutability, a world in which there is no time for pause and reflection:

> This is the ultimate meaning of Ophülsian camera movement: time has no stop. Montage tends to suspend time in the limbo of abstract images, but the moving camera records inexorably the passage of time, moment by moment. As we follow the Ophülsian characters, step by step, up and down stairs, and up and down streets, and round and round the ballroom, we realize their imprisonment in time.[3]

The metaphoric implications of Ophüls' dolly shots can be overlooked, for they are at least to some degree functional: they follow characters in their daily rounds of activities. But a stationary camera could be just

FIG. 16. *La ronde* (1950), directed by Max Ophüls. "There is no escape from the trap of time," Andrew Sarris has observed of the tracking shots in the films of Ophüls. " *'Quelle heure est-il?'* ask the characters in *La ronde,* but it is always too late, and the moment has always passed."

3. "Max Ophüls," in *Interviews with Film Directors,* p. 356.

FIG. 17. *The Earrings of Madame de...(1953)*, directed by Max Ophüls. Sarris has also noted that Ophüls usually tells his stories from the woman's point of view, and "the fluidity of his camera serves to hasten his heroines to their disillusioning rendezvous with reality."

FIG. 18. *The Sins of Lola Montès* (1959), directed by Max Ophüls. "It will all end in a circus," Sarris concludes in his sensitive essay, "with Lola Montès selling her presence to the multitudes, redeeming all men both as a women and as an artistic creation, expressing in one long receding shot the cumulative explosion of the romantic ego for the past two centuries."

The Aesthetic of the Mobile Camera

as functional (not to mention less expensive), for the characters could move toward or away from a fixed set-up (figs. 19, 20). Nor is Ophüls' relentless tracking merely a stylistic affectation as it often seems, for example, in the films of many German directors of the Twenties—for when time is not an important element in a scene, he tends not to use a dolly.

Michelangelo Antonioni combines the ideas of a journey or search with those of time's passing in several dolly shots in *L'avventura*. The notorious reception this movie received at the Cannes Film Festival is somewhat understandable, for the shots often seemed to have no function at all. In scene after scene, the heroine (Monica Vitti) is shown searching over an extinct volcano, along the passageways of a vast mansion, and through the corridors of a hotel. The hostile Cannes audiences kept shouting "Cut! Cut!" They simply could not understand the sheer *duration* of these shots, quite apart from the lack of any pay-off, of some final revelation. Her journey, however, is not so much

FIG. 19. *Wagonmaster* (1950), directed by John Ford. A director's choice of techniques tells us a good deal about his philosophical values. Above all, Ford values a stable community, where dynamic opposites can be reconciled and absorbed.

FIG. 20. *Le plaisir* (1951), directed by Max Ophüls. The philosophic vision of Ophüls, on the other hand, is profoundly concerned with change, with mutability, characteristics which are reflected in his choice of the mobile camera. In the Ophülsian universe, nothing is stable, everything is subject to the degradations of time.

physical as spiritual: she wants to achieve clarity and fulfillment in love. Antonioni uses these lengthy takes to convey *experientially* to the audience the mounting sense of frustration the woman feels in not being able to find some kind of satisfaction; or, to speak metaphorically, in not being able to arrive at her destination. The many corridor images and the occasional traveling shots are used not in a physically functional manner, then, but rather as metaphors of the heroine's symbolic quest, which ultimately leads to her sad discovery of the frailty and transience of love (fig. 21).

The stationary camera tends to convey a sense of stability and order, unless there is a great deal of movement within the frame. The mobile camera—by its very instability—can create ideas of vitality, flux, and sometimes disorder. Orson Welles is fond of exploiting the moving camera to suggest a character's dynamic energy. In his *Othello,* for example, the dolly shot becomes a thematic *motif*. The confident Moor is often photographed in traveling shots, especially at the beginning of the film. In the ramparts scene, he and Iago walk with military brisk-

FIG. 21. *L'avventura* (1960), directed by Michelangelo Antonioni. Because the dolly shot literally travels in space, it is sometimes used to symbolise a journey, a search, or a quest of some kind.

ness, as the camera moves with them at an equally energetic pace. When Iago tells him of his suspicions, the camera slows down, then comes to a halt. Once Othello's mind has been poisoned, he is photographed mostly from stationary set-ups: not only has his confident energy drained away, but a spiritual paralysis invades his soul. In the final shots of the film, he barely moves, even within the still frame. This paralysis *motif* is completed when Othello kills himself.

Because the camera can move in space, a number of film-makers have used crane shots as metaphors of penetration. In the first Susan Alexander sequence of *Citizen Kane,* for example, Welles uses a spectacular crane shot that has been criticised for its showiness by some critics. Through downpouring rain the camera rises to the roof of a seedy nightclub where the wretched Susan is performing, plunges through a neon sign advertising her engagement, then sinks through the skylight of the nightclub, where she has collapsed in a drunken stupor. From a purely functional point of view, Welles could have begun the sequence merely by establishing the scene inside the nightclub, but the shot is not mere virtuosity, as some have claimed. The camera's penetrating movement parallels the reporter's probe into Kane's "real" personality. Both the camera and the reporter encounter numerous obstacles—the rain, the sign, the very walls of the building must be penetrated before we can even see Susan, much less hear her speak. The shot also implies a brutal invasion of privacy, a disregard for the protective psychological barriers Susan has placed around her in her grief.

In *Two Women (La ciociara)* Vittorio De Sica carried the idea of a penetrating camera a step further. The setting is the Second World War in Italy. A mother (Sophia Loren) and her twelve-year-old daughter are on a deserted country road when they pass a bombed-out church. They decide to take a brief rest in the ruin, but shortly after they lie down, they hear strange noises. Suddenly, some screaming Algerian soliders descend upon the two terrified women like screeching birds of prey. The soldiers chase the women and pin them to the ground. One of them mounts the body of the hysterical young girl, and suddenly the camera zooms to a close-up of her agonised face. The zoom shot is a metaphor of sexual penetration. Later in the film, in a shot that has been much criticised and misunderstood by critics, De Sica reverses this shot. The two women are huddled on a bed, weeping over the death of a comrade. Slowly, the camera pulls back, from a medium to long to extreme long shot range, leaving the two women surrounded by an ocean of blackness. In effect, the movement backward is a kind of phallic withdrawal: the scar of the rape, symbolised by the small circle of light (the orginial medium shot) will always remain, but unlike their comrade and thousands of others, the two women have at least survived,they do not dwell in a place of darkness (the surrounding black *matte*).

Godard has expanded the idea of a camera-cum-phallus in an early sequence of *Weekend*. A bourgeois couple sit quietly while the woman recounts a sexual fantasy to her illicit lover. There is virtually no movement within the frame in this very long take: the man calmly listens to the woman's pornographic tale, smokes a cigarette, and occasionally asks a quiet question. Before long, the camera slowly begins to dolly in and out on the static scene, in a motion that can only be described as sluggishly masturbatory. Despite the sardonic wit and audacity of the shot, its effect is eerie and rather melancholy. In the nightmare world of the film, language, like virtually everything else, is perverted from its normal function. In this case, the verbal description of the bizarre sex acts of the woman's story is sexually more statisfying than the sex act itself. Sexual activity in the world of *Weekend* is not a healthy expression of love for others, but a lonely neurotic form of self-stimulation.

The Aesthetic of the Mobile Camera

Perhaps the most far-out and complex use of the mobile camera is found in Bernardo Bertolucci's *Before the Revolution (Prima della revoluzione)*. Mid-way through the film, there is a strange but amusing scene between the young protagonist and an acquaintance, who looks somewhat like Jean-Luc Godard. Their conversation centers almost exclusively on movies. The friend—a film freak if ever there was one—intellectualises on a variety of movies, in the manner of many young European *cinéastes*. He repeats one line of dialogue several times: "The dolly shot is a moral statement." Originally, this comment was made by Godard in reference to the films of Roberto Rossellini. At first, one is inclined to dismiss the statement—indeed, the entire scene—as a typical example of the director's enthusiastic obsession with film culture. Throughout the movie, Bertolucci alludes to a number of films, directors, and cinematic techniques. For that matter, the entire picture is technically very daring, its virtuosity inspired in large part by the works of Godard. The *cinéaste*'s statement, however, is not a gratuitous Godardism, but a verbal clue—communicated in a typically complex, witty and allusive manner—to Bertolucci's theme. This theme is suggested early in the film through the use of the mobile camera.

Like the movies of his idol Godard, Bertolucci's film fuses the themes of contemporary politics and sex. (Stendhal's *The Charterhouse of Parma*, on which the movie is loosely based, also blends these two themes, though in a totally different way.) In the opening dolly shot, we see the protagonist, Fabrizio, running down the streets of Parma, a notoriously reactionary city. The youth is the incarnation of energy and determination, qualities which are emphasised by the swiftly-moving dolly shot. On the soundtrack, we hear his thoughts: he is a Marxist revolutionary, determined to overthrow bourgeois values and reactionary institutions. Throughout the earlier portions of the movie, he is identified with these dynamic traveling shots. Clearly, this is a fervent revolutionary, despite (perhaps because of) his own bourgeois upbringing.

Then Bertolucci introduces Gina, Fabrizio's beautiful young aunt. In a strange and portentous scene, we see her in her bedroom, spreading out a series of photographs on her bed (fig. 22). They seem harmless enough, mostly pictures of herself and family, and a few unfamiliar men. She observes the pictures thoughtfully for some time. The camera then begins to thrust forward and backward, in a masturbatory rhythm that seems rather gratuitous in the political context of the rest of the movie. This masturbatory *motif* is employed in a number of Gina's scenes, even in non-erotic settings.

The aunt and nephew soon engage in a love affair, and before long, the masturbatory movements are used to characterise them both. Lest

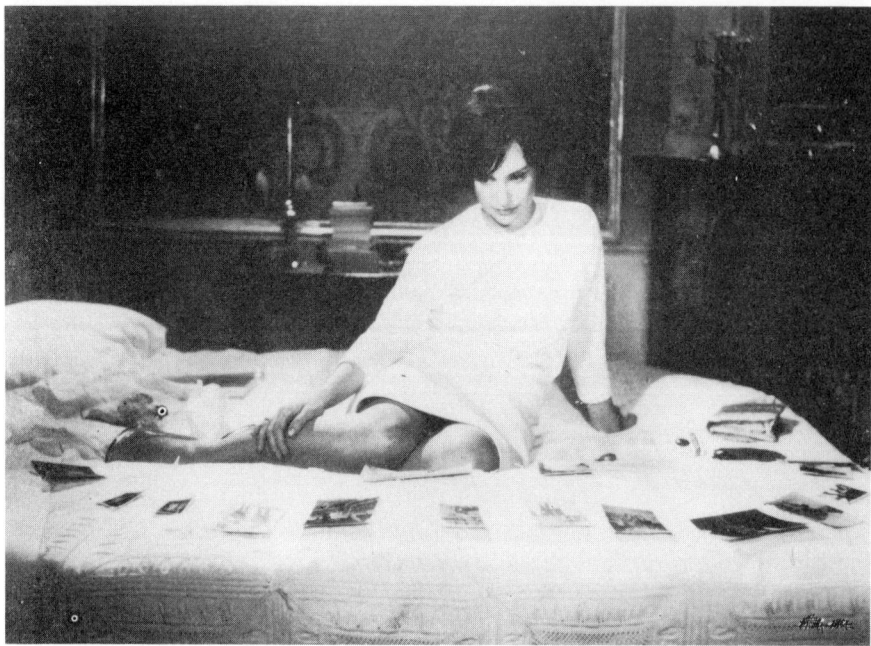

FIG. 22. *Before the Revolution* (1964), directed by Bernardo Bertolucci. The key scene in Bertolucci's film, where the sexual significance of the dolly shots is established for the first time.

the audience miss the point, Bertolucci literally repeats brief traveling shots of Gina and Fabrizio together, almost as though the film clips were instant replays. During the development of the love affair the political theme seems to recede, but in fact a subtle kind of energy transfer has taken place. Fabrizio is no longer characterised by his energetic dolly shots. By virtue of the liaison with his aunt, he is now seen mostly in the masturbatory shots. Although this transfer is not immediately apparent to the audience, Fabrizio's politics have become as incestuous and self-centered as his sex life.

It is at this point that Bertolucci introduces the scene between Fabrizio and his *cinéaste* friend. In what is apparently an allusion to Rossellini's Marxist humanism, the friend tells Fabrizio that "one cannot live without Rossellini." Since Bertolucci provides no context or frame of reference for this scene, its relevance seems dubious. "The dolly shot is a moral statement," the friend repeats cryptically, but within the context of the movie that we, the audience, have been watching, this comment is resonant with thematic implications. The "moral statement" which Bertolucci makes about Fabrizio is, in fact, communicated through dolly shots. The director has condemned the

The Aesthetic of the Mobile Camera

youth for his political self-delusion and hypocrisy: he is far too enamoured of his present life ever to want to change it. Politically, Fabrizio has been jacking off in a fantasy world of Marxist theory, but his real life has been devoted to the pursuit of sensual pleasures. At the end of the film, he recognises that his political commitment, like his incestuous love affair, has been merely an amusing form of self-gratification. In his own words, he has "too much a nostalgia for the present" to want to change the society that provides him with this nostalgia.

As Bertolucci's use of the mobile camera demonstrates, the "point" of a traveling shot is by no means always apparent. Indeed, many viewers are put off by such technical flamboyance in the films of men like Godard and Bertolucci, dismissing it as mere youthful extravagance (as they dismissed it in Welles's films twenty-five years earlier). Certainly there are many instances where the mobile camera is used to cover up the poverty of inspiration of a scene. In Arthur Hiller's *The Hospital*, for example, Paddy Chayefsky's over-verbalised script sim-

FIG. 23. *The Hospital* (1971), directed by Arthur Hiller. Hiller's solution to the problem of a talky and static script proved ultimately unsatisfactory, as the traveling camera, for the most part, was totally unintegrated with the nature of the materials.

ply anchors the visuals to static takes, for the characters never seem to stop talking. In order to suggest *some* kind of action or movement, Hiller uses the mobile camera to photograph many of these scenes (fig.23). But this solution is ultimately unsatisfactory, since the fluid motions of the camera simply distract from the dialogue by implying ideas and emotions that are irrelevant to the scene. Hiller's use of the moving camera is a striking instance of the lack of harmony between form and content in a given situation. In the long run, the film would have been more effective—if less kinetic—if stationary set-ups were used to photograph most of these scenes.

In the hands of a master technician, however, the mobile camera can be superlatively expressive. By and large, traveling shots have been used for functional reasons, probably because of their clumsiness and expense. Because of the obviousness of their purpose, their metaphoric and symbolic implications have often been overlooked. Times have changed, however, especially since the perfection of the hand-held camera. The straitjacket of literalness has been shed at last. Film-makers like Bertolucci and Godard no longer feel the necessity of justifying every camera movement on stricly utilitarian grounds. What has, in fact, evolved is a more sophisticated conception of "function."

3
Cinematic Metaphors

Literature is almost exclusively made up of metaphor, whereas in cinema, metaphor is almost totally absent.
—Pier Paolo Pasolini
The film necessarily leaves behind those characteristic contents of thought which only language can approximate: tropes, dreams, memories, conceptual consciousness.
—George Bluestone
Film in general is not very well suited to abstractions.
—Robert Richardson
What interests me in the cinema is abstraction.
—Orson Welles
Give to the theater and to the novel that which is theirs and to the cinema that which can never belong elsewhere.
—André Bazin

Theoretical Premises

The overwhelming bulk of what's been written about the relationship of film and literature is open to serious question. The two best-known studies, George Bluestone's *Novels into Film*[1] and Robert Richardson's *Literature and Film*,[2] demonstrate an acute sensitivity to

---

1. Reprinted by the University of California Press in 1968. Originally published by the Johns Hopkins Press in 1957.
2. Published in 1969 by the Indiana University Press.

the complexities of literary forms, but a dismaying simplicity of response in dealing with cinematic counterparts. These two critics—like most writers who deal with this subject—are essentially men of letters, and in more ways than one. They write about movies with a certain degree of defensiveness and embarrassment. Indeed, one gains the impression that their film criticism is a naughty but exciting form of intellectual slumming, a harmless diversion from the rigors of "serious" (i.e., literary) criticism. Less sensitive commentators than Bluestone and Richardson have treated the topic of film and literature as a form of artistic one-upmanship: they trot out all the old saws about how literature is more complex, more varied, and more flexible than film (fig. 1); how literature is both concrete and abstract, while movies are "only concrete"; how metaphors are the "soul" of literature (a questionable premise except in poetry, and not always even there), but are totally absent in movies; and so on.

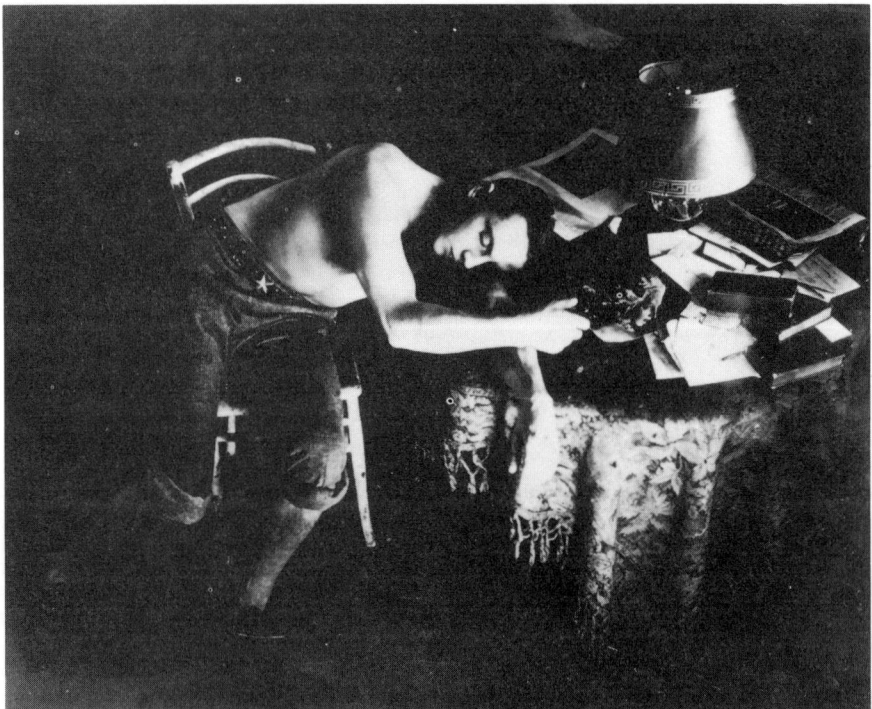

FIG. 1. *Blood of a Poet* (1930), directed by Jean Cocteau. George Bluestone, among others, has claimed that film does not lend itself to portraying dreams. Yet a number of directors—most notably the early surrealists—were attracted to the cinema precisely because of the dream-like nature of the medium.

The theoretical assumptions underlying most of these discussions are based on Siegfried Kracauer's insistence that film is essentially a realistic medium, which, like still photography, shows a marked affinity for recording the objective world around us.[3] That is, the photographic image is a kind of xerography, a literal copy of perceivable objects in nature. The medium of literature, on the other hand, is language—a system of abstract notations which are symbols of objects, feelings, and ideas. Language is conceptual, photography is perceptual. For example, the word "rose" is a mental "image" of something in nature, whereas a photograph of a rose is a literal copy of the object.

In literature, then, language is a necessary intermediary between the reader and the object described. The word "rose" could just as easily be "x," but without some kind of symbolic medium, a writer could not evoke the absent object. The term "imagery" in literature is itself a metaphor: the pictures are seen only by the "mind's eye." The movie image, however, is more direct. It presumably eliminates the intermediary stage of a symbolic medium between the perceiver and the object perceived, since the rose and the picture of the rose are virtually identical.

Theoretically, the immediacy and precision of movie images give film an edge over literature in dealing with concrete subjects, whereas the symbolic flexibility of language gives literature the advantage in dealing with abstractions and non-tangible subjects (fig. 2). The argument runs something like this: a photograph of a red rose is perhaps more vivid and direct than the phrase "a red rose," but only literature can link this image with an abstraction—"my love is like a red rose." Hence, the argument that literature is more supple and complex than cinema because language can symbolise concrete objects and mental states with equal ease. Through the use of metaphors and other figurative devices, literature can be nearly as concrete as film, and far more abstract, since movies are restricted only to those objects which can be photographed. The literalness of photography, its "obligation to representational fidelity," as Bluestone describes it, makes figurative statements difficult if not impossible, for how can film link a concrete object like "rose" with a non-tangible emotion like "love"?

Though this argument has some superficial plausibility, its theoretical premises are faulty. As long ago as 1933, in *Film as Art,* Rudolf Arnheim refuted the simplistic notion that movies are fundamentally

---

3. This is the principal thesis of Kracauer's study, *Theory of Film: The Redemption of Physical Reality* (New York: Oxford University Press, 1960).

FIG. 2. *Juliet of the Spirits* (1965), directed by Federico Fellini. A good argument could be made that fantasies and dreams are *best* rendered in the cinema. The blend of incongruous yet precise details, infinite space, and timelessness is what gives Fellini's fantasy sequences their compelling conviction.

different from any other art form.[4] As a gestalt psychologist, he demonstrated how totally different are the modes of perception of the human eye on the one hand, and the camera's lens on the other. Indeed, Arnheim's principal thesis is that cinematic art is a direct result of these differences in perception. Precisely because of the "limitations" of the photographic medium—that is, its inability to record external reality as it is perceived by the human eye—is the art of the film possible. Art begins where mechanical reproduction leaves off. Like a novelist or a painter, the film director does not copy reality so much as he "imitates" it, in the Aristotelian sense. That is, the film artist translates certain observable characteristics into the *forms* of his

---

4. Arnheim's book was reprinted by the University of California Press in 1957, with additional essays that expand his original thesis.

Cinematic Metaphors

medium. This translation inevitably distorts the original, and it's this distorted "vision" of reality that we value in art, not necessarily how closely the art work resembles the "real thing."

What does all this have to do with metaphors? A great deal, for a metaphor is, among other things, a description that is not literally true. If we grant that film is a literal medium—a copy of reality—we must also grant that the cinema is not a suitable medium for metaphoric expression. But Arnheim established that film does not merely reproduce "what is." Like language in literature, the photographic image in movies is a symbolic intermediary between the audience and the perceived reality. Photography involves many distortions, and from these distortions film directors have created a wide variety of symbols and metaphors. Indeed, the most common cinematic tropes are based on the implied contrast between the ways events are apprehended in reality, and the way that the camera records those events.

In contrasting the perception of the human eye with the camera's lens, Arnheim points out how the very placement of the camera can

FIG. 3. *Monte Carlo* (1930), directed by Ernst Lubitsch. High angle shots often suggest an omnipotent Fate or Destiny, as in this shot, where this idea is reinforced by the symbolism of the roulette table.

distort the object photographed, or how the form of a shot determines its content. If the same man is photographed from a high angle (fig. 3) and then from a low angle, the "information" we receive is different with each shot. Indeed, the shots suggest opposite meanings, though ostensibly the "content" (i.e., the subject matter) is the same. There are a number of other important perceptual differences: we view reality in three dimensions, but film images are two-dimensional. Our experience of space and time is continuous, but movies fragment space and time into segments through the art of editing. Color is either missing or highly distorted in film: even the most "realistic" color processes cannot capture the subtlety and variety of the eye's perception of color in reality. The human eye has a very wide scope of vision, but the movie image is confined within the limited dimensions of the frame. Furthermore, the human eye has no equivalents for such optical modifiers as lenses and filters, or such mechanical distortions as slow motion, reverse motion, fast motion, and freeze frames. Special effects like double and multiple exposure, and negative image have no human ocular counterparts.

Editing Metaphors

Most of the critics who have written about cinematic metaphors have concentrated—if not fixated—on the theory of editing as it was formulated in the Twenties by Vsevolod Pudovkin and Sergei Eisenstein. Pudovkin's theory of associational montage is particularly suited to the creation of metaphors. He postulates that ideas and emotions on film are communicated by the juxtaposition or linking of two or more shots, not by one shot alone. Thus, to return to Burns's simile for a moment, "my love is like a red red rose" could be conveyed cinematically by linking a shot of the loved one with a shot of a rose. David Lean used a variation of this metaphoric comparison in *Doctor Zhivago,* in which a shot of the dreamy hero (accompanied by "Lara's Theme," a musical *motif* for Zhivago's loved one) dissolves to a shot of a field of daffodils, swaying lyrically in the wind, while the musical theme swells grandly.

As Bluestone suggests, however, metaphors of this sort are rather simple-minded when compared to the complexity of most literary metaphors. Not all editing tropes are so obvious, but Pudovkin's linkage technique is severly limited by virtue of its dependence upon setting. That is, any two shots can be yoked together for the purpose of comparison, provided that the contents of the shots are contextually probable. Thus, to take a more sophisticated example of this technique, in Roman Polanski's *Repulsion,* shots of a decaying rabbit

Cinematic Metaphors

carcass on a plate are juxtaposed with shots of the young heroine (Catherine Deneuve), who is slowly descending into madness. The comparison between the girl's deteriorating psyche and the molding rabbit may seem somewhat strained, but because it's literally an object on the set, we accept the comparison as pausible. Literary metaphors of course are usually independent of setting: Burns's comparison does not take place in a garden—the rose image is taken "from nowhere."

Eisenstein believed that Pudovkin was too timid in his use of metaphors, that they were too dependent upon literal plausibility. Eisenstein insisted that film, like literature, could employ "non-naturalistic" tropes—that is, shots that are used in a purely figurative manner, and are not derived from the physical setting of a movie. In *Strike (Stachka),* his first feature, he linked shots of workmen being cut down by machine-guns with shots of cattle being slaughtered. The cattle are not literally on the scene, but are brought in for strictly metaphoric purposes. In *October (Oktyabr;* also known as *Ten Days That Shook the World)* Eisenstein employed non-naturalistic tropes more radically. Shots of Kerensky are juxtaposed with shots of toy jewelled peacocks, and a statue of Napoleon. In a sequence that takes place in a political meeting hall, Eisenstein satirised the timidity of some anti-revolutionary politicians by juxtaposing shots of a fearful platform speaker with shots of an "angelic choir" of harpists. The row of pretty blonde harpists is not intended as a literal representation, but as an ironic metaphor.

In the past decade or so, Eisenstein's metaphoric editing techniques have become more common, most notably in the works of Godard, and perhaps most brilliantly in Bergman's *Persona* (examined in the final section of this essay.) But these techinques have been used in popular as well as "art" films. Stanley Kubrick's *2001: A Space Odyssey,* for example, uses some highly complex metaphors. At the end of the first episode, some anthropoid apes discover that thigh bones can be used as weapons—in effect, as primitive machines. At the close of the sequence, the ape leader joyously hurls the thigh bone into the air. We see a close-up of the bone as it floats in slow motion. Kubrick then cuts to a shot of a long sleek spaceship shaped like the bone, traveling effortlessly through space. The linked shots suggest a technological metaphor: the primitive intelligence that devised the weapon/machine of the bone has evolved into the sophisticated intelligence that has created the spaceship in the year 2001.

Kubrick expands this metaphor in the final third of the film, which takes place "beyond Jupiter." The intelligence on Jupiter has captured the astronaut and kept him in a kind of laboratory-cum-zoo-cum-Louis XV apartment. After he dies, we see an embryo-planet floating in the cosmos: the embryo has the facial features of the astronaut. Kubrick suggests metaphorically that the "star child" is to the intelligence on Jupiter as the spaceship was to Twenty-First-century man, and the thigh bone to the primordial ape. Metaphorically, Kubrick also implies that man's next evolutionary leap in intelligence will *begin* at an embryonic stage, relative to the kind of intelligence that's found on Jupiter. The metaphor is deliberately ambiguous, suggesting on the one hand that man will be the tool or machine of the higher intelligence on Jupiter, and on the other, that with the help of this intelligence, man will surpass himself.

Virtually all discussions of editing tropes are content-oriented. The metaphorical implications of other aspects of editing are ignored . For example, the rhythm of a sequence of spliced shots can be just as important as the subject matter of the shot. In Leni Riefenstahl's *Triumph of the Will (Triumph des Willens),* for instance, many of the shots are edited to a military beat, and the relentless rhythm conveys a sense of precision and inexorability which is totally appropriate to the propogandist purpose of the film—the exaltation of Nazi ideals.

Through a series of shock cuts—the rapid juxtaposition of shots — the film director can deliberately disorient an audience. Such techniques are often used to convey metaphorically the sense of dislocation and fragmentation which results from violence and confusion, as can be seen in the famous shower sequence from Hitchcock's *Psycho* and throughout much of Bergman's *Persona*. In other contexts, shock cutting can suggest the spontaneity and whimsy of a character or group of characters, as can be seen in the Beatles films of Richard Lester.

The duration and placement of shots can also be used metaphorically. In *The Pawnbroker,* Sidney Lumet intercut short flashback scenes with present-tense sequences to suggest the experience of psychological repression. The protagonist (Rod Steiger) is a middle-aged Jew who survived a Nazi concentration camp twenty-five years earlier. He now owns a pawnshop in Spanish Harlem, and has dedicated his life to obliterating all memories of the past. His efforts, however, are constantly frustrated by events in the present acting as continual reminders. The present-tense sequences are interrupted by flickering inserts, some six or eight frames long. We cannot discern the contents of these flashing intrusions, but we do experience a desire to permit the idea or feeling of the shot to find some kind of "release." These flickering interruptions recur for progessively longer intervals, until we recognise that the contents of these shots are set in the past. Eventually, the present is totally suspended and a past-tense sequence takes over. Rather than simply dissolve or cut to a flashback, Lumet uses this flickering technique as a metaphor of the protagonist's desire

Cinematic Metaphors

to repress his memories—a struggle that his conscious mind loses in a matter of seconds.

Since editing destroys the continuity of actual time, a number of metaphorical ideas have been derived from this artificial fragmentation. The flash-forward, for example, invariably suggests ideas of fate and predestination, since we literally see events that have not yet occurred. In Sydney Pollack's *They Shoot Horses, Don't They?*, the present-tense story is interrupted by shots of the past and the future (fig. 4.) The future-tense scenes show fragments of the young protagonist (Michael Sarrazin) being arrested, arraigned, and tried in court. Yet the present offers no explanation of the future until late in the film, when we see him shoot a wretchedly dejected girl (Jane Fonda) in a compassionate gesture of mercy. The flash-forwards are metaphors of a hostile determinism—of a future as rigged as the dance hall marathon which is the setting for the movie.

The meaning of any given shot is determined as much by what is left

FIG. 4. *They Shoot Horses, Don't They?* (1969), directed by Sydney Pollack. Unlike flash-backs, flash-forwards are rarely employed in film. Pollack's flash-forwards are used as metaphors of a hostile Fate, of a future that is totally predetermined before it occurs.

out as by what is included. Editing chops up the continuity of space into a sequence of separate space "blocks," thus permitting the film-maker to exploit the spatial fragmentation for metaphorical purposes. In *Alice's Restaurant,* for example, Arthur Penn is concerned with the thematic polarities of isolation and community. The communal scenes are photographed predominantly in long shots, which permit a number of people to share the same frame (space). Ideas of loneliness and alienation are suggested through the exploitation of close-ups, which isolate individuals in separate space fragments. This technique is particulary effective in the marriage scene late in the film. After a tense period of mutual resentment and hostility, Alice and Ray Brock decide to reaffirm their bond by marrying again in a communal hippie ceremony. Ordinarily, a marriage ceremony would be photographed either in a long shot, or a medium range two-shot, for the essence of such a scene is the idea of an intimate bond between two individuals, two people sharing the same area or space. Instead, Penn shoots the marriage ceremony in a series of separate close-ups, suggesting metaphorically that Alice and Ray are permanently estranged, despite the apparent unification of the ceremony.

Editing tropes, then, are not restricted merely to the subject matter of two linked shots. Montage distorts our literal perception of space and time, and from these distortions, film-makers have created a wide variety of metaphors. Furthermore, montage tropes are merely one class of figurative devices that are used in movies. The majority of cinematic metaphors are found within a single set-up, not between two or more linked shots.

Aural, Kinetic, and Optical Metaphors

A serious shortcoming of most commentators who have discussed the relationship of film to literature is their tendency to reduce cinematic techniques to literary counterparts. In some cases, the parallels are apt, but often the complexities of film are outrageously oversimplified. For example, many years ago, the film historian Terry Ramsaye referred to editing as the "syntax of film." Ramsaye was speaking metaphorically, but a surprising number of subsequent critics interpreted his remark literally and never bothered to differentiate between the syntax of words and the "syntax" of movie images. A typical instance of the tendency to point out literary and cinematic "parallels" is in Robert Richardson's *Literature and Film:*

> The vocabulary of film is the simple photographed image; the grammar and

syntax of film are the editing, cutting, or montage process by which the shots are arranged. Single shots have meaning much as single words do, but a series of carefully arranged shots conveys meaning much as a composed phrase does. (p. 65)

To the literature-oriented reader, such statements have apparently seemed reasonable, for they have been repeated with monotonous regularity ever since the Twenties. But to anyone who has thought seriously about film images—or, for that matter, about *any* kind of visual image—observations of this sort seem incredibly naive. To be sure, "single words" in the right context can be rich and resonant, but no matter how complex a word, it can't be compared to even a banal shot from a sleazy movie, for film images by necessity include many elements.

Charles Barr contemptuously dismisses most analogies between literature and film precisely because of this tendency to reduce the "content" of movie images to a simple-minded "x." As Barr points out, words evoke details sequentially, even though the subject matter exits simultaneously: there is no literary equivalent for "getting things in the same shot."[5] This is a crucial distinction, and too many commentators, including some film directors, have either forgotten it or never noticed it in the first place, in their crude attempts to force analogies between words and images. As Barr says, "How else can you translate 'the cat sat on the mat' into film except in a single shot?" (p.323) Even the "simplest" movie images, then, are more complicated than any one given word, for a shot necessarily involves not only the multiplicities of subject matter, but also the framing, angle, lighting, texture, focus, and so on. When one speaks of an artistically complex image—one of Josef von Sternberg's richly evocative shots from *The Scarlet Empress,* for example—the analogies between image and word become even more ludicrous (fig.5). It would take many paragraphs for a sensitive writer to capture all the nuances of Sternberg's image. No one in his right mind would suggest that a word—or even a paragraph or many pages of words—is "analogous" to a fine painting. Yet many critics blithely continue to equate words with film images, despite the fact that individual shots from movies can be fully as complex and rich as a good painting.

It is this very complexity of film images that makes detailed criticism difficult in the cinema. Film critics can't really "quote." In order to point out a detail from a shot, the movie critic often must devote many

---

5. "CinemaScope: Before and After," in *Film : A Montage of Theories,* edited by Richard Dyer MacCann (New York: E. P. Dutton, 1966), p. 323.

FIG. 5. *The Scarlet Empress* (1934), directed by Josef von Sternberg. To equate a cinematic shot with a word or phrase is a ridiculous simplification of the complexity of movie images, particularly images created by such masters of *mise-en-scène* as Sternberg.

sentences—sometimes paragraphs—to place the detail in its visual and dramatic context. No wonder most critics prefer to ignore form and technique in film: it's much easier simply to talk about "subject matter" in a general sense. No doubt the reason most critics have restricted their discussions of metaphor to editing tropes is because they believe that a single shot yoked to another is the equivalent to yoking together two words, or at best, two phrases. Indeed, montage tropes are often hackneyed precisely because of the crudeness of this technique in film. Images simply don't link as easily as words, because images are more complex, more densely saturated with information, more ambiguous. Because of this greater complexity, most cinematic metaphors are found within single shots, not between two or more of them.

Before discussing what some of these metaphoric techniques are, we ought to distinguish between metaphors and symbols. In the criticism of the past few years—both literary and cinematic—there has been a tendency to use the two terms interchangeably. There has always been much overlapping between the two terms, and the differences are even more blurred in film than in literature, as we shall see in the discussion of *Psycho* and *Persona*. But for the moment certain useful distinctions ought to be preserved.

A symbol can be defined as something that represents something else, as well as being a thing in itself. It is a contextually plausible detail which, in a given framework, emerges as meaning something in additon to what it literally represents. For example, in Welles's *Citizen Kane*, the snow-sled "Rosebud" is literally a child's toy; in the context of the movie, it also emerges as a symbol of Kane's lost innocence and childhood. The symbolic meaning of the sled is an *extension* of its literal meaning. In a strict sense, the toy is not a metaphor. Movies can employ symbols with great density. Indeed, next to spoken language, the most common method of dealing with abstract ideas in film is through symbolism. Lighting, objects, colors, costumes, settings—all of these and many more have been exploited for symbolic purposes. The important distinction to be made about symbolism is that it emerges unobtrusively from the context of a film. Like symbolism in literature, it's quite possible for a symbol in movies not be to noticed, for its "thingness" permits it to exist independently.

Metaphors, on the other hand, usually strike us with a sense of incongruity. A metaphor can be defined as a comparison of some kind that isn't literally true. A term is transferred from an object or idea it ordinarily describes to another object or idea. The phrase "sluttish time," for example, connects the abstraction "time" with incongruous ideas that are ordinarily associated with brothels, cheapness, and lack of passion. Virtually all metaphors (both cinematic and literary) have symbolic implications, then, for a metaphoric description is true only in a figurative (i.e., symbolic) sense.

Arnheim's theory is perhaps the best foundation for a discussion of cinematic tropes, for he stresses the differences between our perception of phenomena in the real world and the distortions of these phenomena by the camera and projector. Because movie images are enclosed within a frame, the film-maker can exploit the space within and outside the frame for metaphorical purposes. Generally, what exists inside the frame is in some kind of light; outside of it is the darkness of the theater. This darkness can be exploited to convey emotions dealing with fear, the unknown, obscurity —in short, all the symbolic ideas traditionally associated with darkness and the lack of light (fig.6). By placing a character at the edge of the frame, the director can create metaphors of that character's nearness to death, oblivion,

FIG. 6. *Macbeth* (1971), directed by Roman Polanski. The darkness outside the frame can be used for metaphorical purposes, since darkness is often associated with evil, insecurity, and death. In this shot, Macbeth has just murdered the King and is showing the bloody daggers to Lady Macbeth.

and so on. In the first scene of Godard's *Masculine-Feminine,* the protagonist Paul is kept at the edge of the frame, where he seems in constant danger of slipping off into the darkness—a visual forshadowing of his death at the end of the film.

Different portions of the screen can convey metaphoric ideas, for various areas tend to suggest intrinsic ideas and emotions. In a long shot of a solitary man standing on a hill, for example, the director can suggest exultation and god-like omnipotence by exploiting the height of the screen (i.e., by placing the man near the top of the frame), or he can suggest vulnerability and insignificance by placing the man and hilltop near the bottom of the screen (fig. 7), thus permitting the vastness of the skies to fill most of the area inside the frame.

The amount of space permitted within the frame is also an important source of metaphors. A tightly framed shot generally does not permit much latitude of movement, for all of the objects and people within the frame are balanced with some degree of precision. A loosely framed

FIG. 7. *Zabriskie Point* (1969), directed by Michelangelo Antonioni. The placement of objects within the frame is a common source of metaphors and symbols in the cinema. The two figures in this shot are placed near the bottom of the frame—a position of vulnerability and danger.

shot permits considerable movement within a given space. Tight framing is usually—though not always—associated with close shots, loose framing with long shots. Directors have used this kind of space manipulation to suggest metaphors of freedom and entrapment. Laurence Olivier's film treatment of *Hamlet* is about "a man who could not make up his mind," as the opening title informs us. Appropriately, Olivier used mostly loosely-framed long shots in his film. Hamlet has considerable freedom of movement, but he refuses to use it, preferring instead to sulk in dark corners. In Tony Richardson's version of the play, Hamlet is characterised as a frustrated and impulsive man. Appropriately, the film is shot almost exclusively in confining close-ups, with the tortured Hamlet virtually spilling over the edges of the frame into "oblivion" (fig. 8). The unstable hand-held camera can barely keep up with him as he lunges impulsively from place to place. Even with the same "content," then, directors can project opposing interpretations of a character and situation merely by stressing different spatial metaphors. Framing metaphors are uniquely cinematic, for

FIG. 8. *Hamlet* (1969), directed by Tony Richardson. The amount of space that a director permits his actors within the frame is often used metaphorically. Throughout his film, Richardson "imprisons" his protagonist, confining him almost exclusively to medium and close shots.

even though the legitimate theater is in part a visual medium, the "frame" size (the confines of the set, or the proscenium arch) remains the same for the duration of the play. The theater in short, is restricted to "long shots."

Other kinds of movements can also be exploited for metaphoric purposes. Perhaps the most obvious examples of kinetic tropes can be found in films dealing with dance—musicals, for example. Virtually any dance number is a stylised metaphoric expression of emotions and ideas. In some instances, kinetic metaphors can include objects as well as dancers. In George Sidney's *Pal Joey*, for example, the reawakening of love in a cynical, worldly matron (Rita Hayworth) is expressed through a series of aural and visual juxtapositions. The morning after a sexual liaison, she rises from her bed and sings the song, "Bewitched, Bothered, and Bewildered." As she begins, she walks to a set of louvered windows, and absently clicks open two or three louvers. As the number progresses, she opens up the whole shutter, then another, and finally a series of doors, as the tune reaches its conclusion. The *motif* of openings—from small individual louvers to huge swinging doors—suggests metaphorically the "opening up" of her world through love. In this context the progressive expansiveness of the *motif* is also a witty sexual metaphor.

Other tropes involving movement can be formed through the manipulation of the camera's speed mechanism. Fast and slow motion are probably the most important sources of tropes of this kind. In slow motion sequences, all movements are reduced to a dreamy dance-like gracefulness. Time is sometimes torturously elongated, as in the hallucinatory nightmare sequence from Luis Buñuel's *Los olvidados*, where a woman holds up a huge chunk of raw meat, which throbs and undulates eerily as a result of the slow motion photography. Scenes of destruction and murder can take on a strangely beautiful, balletic elegance, as in many of the violent episodes of Sam Peckinpah's *The Wild Bunch*.

Fast motion is particularly suitable for metaphors dealing with chaos, lack of control, and mechanisation. When screen events take place at a much faster rate than they do in life, dignity is difficult, and the result is almost invariably comic. Richard Lester's *A Hard Day's Night* used fast motion to suggest the wild spontaneity of the Beatles and the disrupting effect they have on others. In the Upton Inn sequence of *Tom Jones*, Tony Richardson used this technique to convey metaphorically the mechanical predictability of all the characters: the scene's breakneck speed suggests a machine gone beserk.

Oddly enough, few directors have used reverse motion for creating metaphors in film. For the most part, this technique is used simply for a gag—a laugh for its own sake, as in Lester's *The Knack*, where an egg "returns" to its shell. Reverse motion, however, is rich in metaphoric possibilities, for it can suggest the erasing of time and events, a return to the past, and the idea of Fate, since—like the flashback—reverse motion permits us to see the past unfolding in the present, only literally. In a stunningly evocative sequence of *Orpheus (Orphée)*, Jean Cocteau used slow and reverse motion simultaneously, to suggest the dream-like unreality of the setting (the Hell of the imagination), and the protagonist's return to the past and to a more innocent previous condition.

Freeze frames—the negation of movement in film—are often used to create metaphors dealing with time and space. By "freezing" (itself a metaphor) the contents of a shot, a director can suggest a halting of time and physical change. Henry Hathaway used a freeze frame effectively at the end of *True Grit*, in a shot where the protagonist (John Wayne) and his horse leap over a fence. By freezing the shot on the crest of the leap, Hathaway creates a metaphor of timeless grandeur:

the shot suggests a heroic equestrian statue, immune from the ravages of time and decay. The total absence of movement is often associated with death, and Hathaway's freeze frame also suggests this idea. Perhaps a more explicit metaphor of death can be seen in the conclusion of George Roy Hill's *Butch Cassidy and the Sundance Kid,* where the two protagonists (Paul Newman and Robert Redford) are "frozen" just before they are shot to death. But like Hathaway's freeze frame, Hill's suggests a kind of ultimate triumph over death. As in Shakespeare's sonnets, art— in this case, the freeze frame, which eternalises the protagonists—represents a triumph over the forces of mutability and death.

In *The Pumpkin Eater,* Jack Clayton used freeze frames to suggest the permanence of the past. The heroine (Anne Bancroft) recalls the events leading up to her present misery in a series of flashbacks, each of which ends in a freeze frame. The freezing of these shots conveys metaphorically the unalterability of the past: like so many frozen fragments of time, the events of her past have sealed off any possibility of realtering the present. Her psychological paralysis is further emphasised by her rigid posture in the present: like a chic mannequin, her body seems stiff, devoid of energy, incarcerated in its fashionable clothing.

Many kinetic metaphors are created through the use of the moving camera. The speed with which a camera dollys can be a metaphor of psychic and moral energy in a character. In *Citizen Kane,* we often see the idealistic, enthusiastic young Kane in brisk traveling shots. As he grows older and more corrupt, the dolly shots grow slower and more deliberate. When Kane is an old man, he is virtually immobile, and is photographed primarily in stationary set-ups, suggesting a kind of moral stagnation.

The direction of a dolly shot's movement can also be employed metaphorically. In *The Earrings of Madame de...* Max Ophüls employed a circular *motif* in his dolly shots, especially in the ballroom dancing scenes. This circular *motif* parallels the structure of the film, which follows a pair of earrings from husband to wife, wife to pawnshop, pawnshop to lover, and finally, lover to mistress—who is the original wife!

Through the use of non-synchronous sound, the film director can create a number of metaphors by contrasting his visuals with a sound that has no source within the frame. This contrasting technique can be used with dialogue, sound effects, and music. In *Accident,* Joseph Losey used a non-synchronous dialogue sequence to create a metaphor of alienation, deception, and loneliness. A middle-aged college don (Dirk Bogarde) decides to look up a former mistress when he

Cinematic Metaphors

visits London. Through a rain-streaked window, we see the two eating silently in a dingy restaurant (fig. 9). On the soundtrack, we hear a conversation between them, apparently their first social exchange when the man entered her apartment. Their dialogue is strained and evasive, filled with awkward pauses and stretches of silence. By juxtaposing this conversation with the non-synchronous visuals, Losey suggests that the statements of the characters are "detached" from their actions—the central theme of the movie, which was scripted by Harold Pinter.

Sound effects can also be used metaphorically. Bergman's *The Shame (Skammen)* traces the gradual degeneration of a married couple who live in a country engaged in a civil war. The war has dragged on for so long, the two are eventually numbed into insensibility as horror is piled upon horror. In one sequence, their house and farm are bombed to shreds. After the two withdraw from the rubble of their former home, they survey the damage to their farm: the trees and vegetation

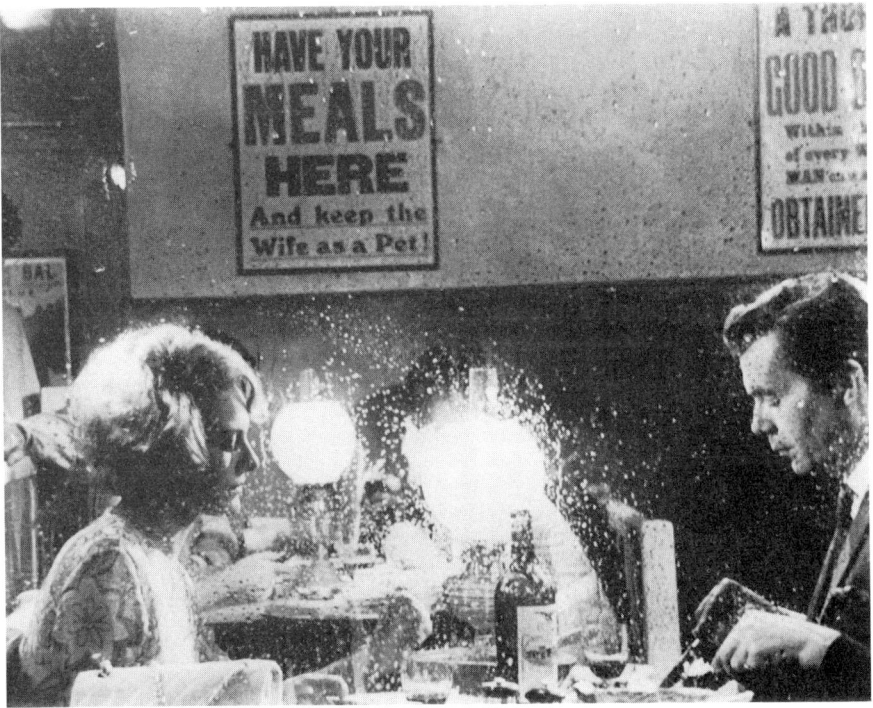

FIG. 9. *Accident* (1967), directed by Joseph Losey. In a bleak, melancholy sequence of this film, Losey juxtaposed this shot with a non-synchronous soundtrack of a conversation between these two silent diners, producing a weird sense of "disconnectedness."

have been blasted beyond recognition. The two look at the charred *débris* apparently without passion: they are too drained for emotional response. But on the soundtrack, the remorseless echo of dripping drops of water can be heard. The dripping sound has no visual source, but is used as a metaphor for the tears the two are too exhausted to cry.

A number of directors have used music in a "literary" way, to make a comment on the visuals, often ironic. In *2001*, Kubrick used Richard Strauss's tone poem "Thus Spake Zarathustra," a composition inspired by Nietzsche's philosophical tract heralding the coming of the Superman. Kubrick employs the beginning of this music to accompany those scenes which depict a giant leap in the evolution of intelligence, towards the creation of a Superman. Kubrick also employs music for ironic and witty contrasts, as in the sequence where the Twenty-First-century spaceship glides through the blueness of space to the

FIG. 10. *Blonde Venus* (1932), directed by Josef von Sternberg. Throughout the Thirties, Paramount Pictures tended to favor images with a shimmering elegance. Sternberg was particularly brilliant in his use of filters to lend mystery, elegance, or sparkle to his images.

Cinematic Metaphors

accompaniment of Johann Strauss's Ninteteeth-century "Blue Danube" waltz. The music is funny primarily because of the initial sense of incongruity. But—more subtly— Kubrick is also in dead earnest, for in the infinity of time and space the magnificent intellectual achievements of the year 2001 appear rather quaintly old-fashioned in comparison to what lies ahead in the cosmos beyond Jupiter.

The majority of cinematic metaphors are found in the texture of the film image itself. Many of these metaphors are mechanically produced by the optical printer and by such distorting modifiers as lenses and filters (figs. 10, 11). Bo Widerberg's *Elvira Madigan* is a good example of how filters can totally alter the surfaces of realty. The golden haze that gave the scenes their lush glow was not merely an attempt to prettify the film, but to force the audience to share, at least temporarily, the extravagantly romantic "vision" of the two central characters (fig. 12).

There are dozens of lenses that can alter the camera's recording of a scene. In *Long Day's Journey into Night*, Sidney Lumet used specific lenses for each of the four main characters, and these lenses changed

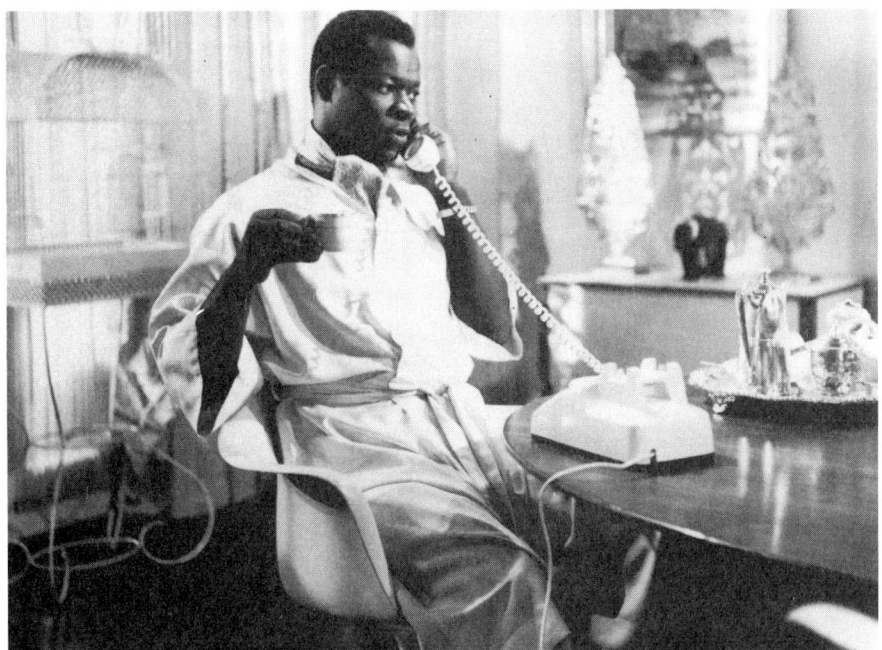

FIG. 11. *The Pawnbroker* (1965), directed by Sidney Lumet. Some directors use filters to parody the "elegance" of the studio films of the Thirties. In this shot, Lumet seems to be mocking the phony glamor of the lighting, costumes and set designs of such films.

FIG. 12. *Elvira Madigan* (1967), directed by Bo Widerberg. Widerberg's film was widely praised for its lush romanticism, which was achieved in great part through his elaborate use of filters.

FIG. 13. *Long Day's Journey into Night* (1962), directed by Sidney Lumet. In this film, Lumet used a variety of lenses to suggest individual psychological states. In the early part of the movie, he used non-distorting lenses to suggest the relative tranquility of the family scenes. Once this serenity has been shattered, each member of the family is photographed by a "characteristic" lens.

as the characters developed during the course of the film (fig. 13). Lumet refers to this complex use of lenses as a "lens plot." For the morphine-addicted mother (Katharine Hepburn), Lumet used a series of progressively longer (telephoto) lenses, which blur the background into a fuzzy remoteness: a metaphor of how the drugs are helping her to forget or at least blur the world around her. For the weary father (Ralph Richardson) and the cynical older son (Jason Robards), Lumet used progressively wider angled lenses, which intensify and exaggerate depth perception. The distortion of depth that these lenses produce suggests how Mary Tyrone's addiction has distorted their own lives. Only Edmund (Dean Stockwell), the naive younger son, is photographed with a conventional lens, suggesting his (relative) normality, though he too is characterised through a wide angle lens later in the film, after he realises (as his father and brother had much earlier) that their situation is without hope.[6]

The amount of distortion in wide angle lenses varies considerably (fig. 14). The wider the angle, the greater the distortion. In *Touch of Evil,* Welles used extreme wide angle lenses to photograph a murder scene. Some of the shots are close-ups of Welles, in which his nose is exploded into a huge bulb and his eyes narrowed to sinister slits. As photographed, the scene is intensely grotesque: in a tawdry, steaming hotel room, the two fat men—murderer and victim—charge and heave like two prehistoric animals. The rapidly-edited sequence is lit in harsh contrasts and photographed from extreme angles. On the soundtrack, we hear the animal-like grunts and squeals of the attacker and victim.

Even the quality of the lighting and film stock can be used metaphorically (fig. 15). In *Faces,* for example, John Cassavetes used fast stock for most of the sequences, resulting in a grainy image texture that was further emphasised when the film was blown up from 16mm to 35mm (fig. 16). One sequence was shot with conventional slow stock, however, and lit in a rather old fashioned studio manner. This scene has a glossy, slick surface that contrasts noticeably with the gritty surfaces of the other scenes. It is the "morning after" sequence when the adulterous husband (John Marley) dreamily imagines that he can begin his life anew with his prostitute girl-friend. The unreality of the middle-aged executive's pipe-dream is communicated metaphorically, by the "glamorous" image surface. Visually, the scene seems to be pure fantasy, a delusion that the husband himself later acknowledges sadly.

---

6. See Dale Luciano's excellent interview,*"Long Day's Journey into Night: An Interview with Sidney Lumet,"* in *Film Quarterly* (Fall, 1971), pp. 20-29.

FIG. 14. *Deliverance* (1972), directed by John Boorman. Because of its distortion of perspective, the wide angle lens is often used to suggest symbolic psychological distances rather than literal ones.

FIG. 15. *The Last Picture Show* (1971), directed by Peter Bogdanovich. Metaphors and symbols can be created by fortuitous accidents during shooting. Bogdanovich photographed one scene in his film in a long take: as the character (Ben Johnson) reminisces wistfully about a long past love affair, the sun suddenly bursts through the gloomy Texas skies, showering the speaker with a sudden radiance.

FIG. 16. *Faces* (1968), directed by John Cassavetes. High-speed film produces a graininess in the image, and when this graininess is very severe, the subject photographed sometimes seems to be disintegrating.

In *The Passion of Anna (En passion)*, Bergman exploited the graininess of fast stock to create a metaphor of psychological disintegration. The central character (Max von Sydow) is torn between emotional indifference, which means isolation and loneliness, and the continuation of a love affair that has soured, which will bring emotional chaos and perhaps even gradual self-destruction. The movie ends with a shot of the indecisive protagonist pacing back and forth on a lonely road. Beginning from an extreme long shot position, the camera slowly zooms in to a closer view of the scene. As it does so, the graininess of the image (which is magnified by the lens) becomes more pronounced. By the time the camera stops zooming, all we see of the man is a blob of moving dots—he seems to disintegrate before our eyes.

Certain optical effects are particularly suited to the creation of metaphors. Dissolves, double, and multiple exposures literally superimpose two or more realities simultaneously. The opening sequence of *Citizen Kane* is composed of a number of dissolving shots of fences and impediments which surround Xanadu, Kane's opulent palace. The dissolves suggest a series of layers of protection that the camera is able to penetrate in its movement towards the castle. These layer metaphors are parellel to the psychological barriers that Kane uses to protect and isolate himself; the camera's penetration of these layers is analogous to the reporter's penetration of the enigma of Kane's personality.

There was a time when double or multiple exposures were used primarily in scenes dealing with the supernatural, but a number of directors have expanded their use. In *All Fall Down,* for example, John Frankenheimer used a series of multiple exposures in a lyrical scene depicting two lovers (Warren Beatty and Eva Marie Saint) kissing passionately. The scene functions on a number of levels: it suggests the passage of time; the dissolving effect suggests a merging of the two bodies (i.e., it's a metaphor of romantic union); and the slow craning in from a long shot position to close-up range seems to be a metaphor of sexual penetration (a more appropriate symbol than those used during the Thirties and Forties, when during such scenes, the camera would "discreetly" pan or tilt away, leaving the audience totally confused as to whether or not the lovers ever managed to consummate their union).

In the hey-day of the studio years in Hollywood, optical transitions—especially wipes—were fashionable. Most of these rather flashy techniques were used as gimmicks, but some directors have integrated the metaphoric implications of wipes into the themes of their films. In *Throne of Blood (Kumonosu-jo),* Akira Kurosawa's loose adaptation of *Macbeth,* the wipe is used as a transition between a number of short scenes showing the protagonist (Toshiro Mifune) lost in a dense forest. He and his lieutenant gallop furiously from one location to another, but they merely manage to entangle themselves further in the bowels of the forest. The wipe transitions suggest the inexorable determination of the protagonist to erase his miscalculations; they are metaphors of his ruthless but blundering ascent to power. Kurosawa's wipes are simple vertical lines that travel across the screen, pushing one image off and pulling in another. Clock wipes (a circular movement of a line that travels like the hand of a clock) have been used to suggest the rapid passing of time; flip-overs to imply the zany topsy-turviness of a dramatic embroglio; spiral wipes to suggest psychological penetration or the sensation of vertigo; and so on. In short, when they are integrated into the theme or characterisation of a flim, wipes can suggest a wide variety of metaphorical ideas.

The iris is another sadly-neglected optical technique. By irising in on a subject, a film-maker can encircle it with a symbolic shroud of blackness (fig. 17). In Welles's nostalgic *The Magnificent Ambersons,* a sentimental scene depicting a country drive in a primitive open-air automobile concludes with a shot of the auto chugging precariously

FIG. 17. *Intolerance* (1916), directed by D. W. Griffith. A master of every type of masking shot, Griffith often used the iris to encircle a significant detail with a symbolic sea of darkness. In this scene, the protagonist is about to be executed by hanging.

over a hilltop in extreme long shot. As it crests the hill, the car is enclosed by an iris, creating an antique effect, like a frayed family photograph, or a cameo-shaped brooch. The black *matte* surrounding the vehicle suggests the impending snuffing out of such carefree scenes from the Amberson's future, and the end of a slower, more graceful way of life for the country at large.

In general, negative images have been avoided by most directors as too showy and distracting. A number of American Underground film-makers have explored the metaphoric possibilties of this technique, and in *Alphaville,* Godard used it for an x-ray effect, a looking beneath the surface of reality. Because of its eerie reversals of dark and light, most directors have used negative images for metaphors dealing with death and the supernatural. Jean Cocteau's *Testament of Orpheus (Le testament d'Orphée),* for instance, features a shot of an Angel of Death in negative image.

Film color has generally been used for symbolic rather than metaphoric purposes. Since the early Sixties, however, several directors haved used color non-naturalistically. In the credit sequence of Hitchcock's *Topaz* hundreds of Soviet soldiers march past the camera;

virtually everything in this sequence—tanks, streets, skies, people—is reduced to monochromatic variations of bluish gray, an appropriately drab color for a drab society. Only the Soviet red stars on the helmets and caps of the soldiers "enliven" the surface of the images—a typical instance of Hitchcock's ironic and malicious wit. Antonioni's famous "adjustments" of natural locales in *Red Desert (Deserto rosso)* represented an important advance in the metaphorical use of color. He simply spray-painted whatever did not suit his particular needs: trees and swamps were painted gray, fruit and streets stark white, white walls turned pink before our eyes, and so on. *Red Desert* opened up a whole range of possibilities in the use of "artificial" (i.e., metaphoric) colors in films.

Reality, then, can be tampered with. After it has been adjusted to suit a metaphorical purpose, the camera records it and it becomes "true," even though we know that literally the photographed scene doesn't exist in nature (fig. 18). Special effects ("trick") photography

FIG. 18. *Beauty and the Beast* (1946), directed by Jean Cocteau. "The more one touches mystery," Cocteau once observed, "the more important it becomes to be realistic."

Cinematic Metaphors

is particularly rich in metaphoric possibilities, as Jean Cocteau's Orpheus Trilogy demonstrates (fig. 19). In the first film of the trilogy, *Blood of a Poet (Le sang d'un poète),* an artist plunges into a mirror and enters the weird world of poetic creation. He wakes to find a scar-mouth on his hand, which both fascinates and repels him: the poetic faculty is both a grotesque deformity and an inspired gift of expression. The poet later becomes a stone statue, which turns to snow. Callous schoolboys use the statue's snow to make snowballs with, while he looks on in helpless horror. The poet blows his brains out with a gun, and the flowing blood transforms into a laurel wreath. From the lodge of a fashionable theater, patrons applaud the poet's suicide: his pain produces pleasure in others. Cocteau's literalised metaphors have not been widely imitated in the commerical cinema, but his greatest disciple, Jean-Luc Godard, has explored many of the implicatiions of these poetic techniques, particularly in *Pierrot le fou, Weekend,* and *Vladimir and Rosa.*

FIG. 19. *Testament of Orpheus* (1959), directed by Jean Cocteau. In discussing metaphor in film, virtually all commentators neglect the enormous potential of special effects photography. Cocteau's poetic masterpieces would have been impossible without these techniques.

Psycho and *Persona*

In actual practice, the problems of symbolic meaning in film are infinitely more complex than this brief survey would suggest. In the cinema even more than in literature, the distinctions between symbols and metaphors can seem merely academic, for these terms have a way of merging imperceptibly while actually watching a movie. Earlier, we defined a symbol as an object or event that means something in addition to what it literally represents. The symbolic object always retains its non-abstract quality, its contextual integrity—like Kane's snow-sled. A metaphor we defined as a somewhat incongruous element in film, something that is less integrated contexually, less "realistic" in terms of our ordinary perceptions. Metaphors, then, are more obtrusive — more stylised and self-conscious—than symbols.

Perhaps this degree of obtrusiveness is the most pragmatic method of differentiating between the four major types of symbolic communication in film: *motifs,* symbols, metaphors, and allegory. Instead of locking each of these terms into an air-tight compartment, however, we ought to view them as general demarcations on a *continuous* spectrum, with *motifs* representing the least obtrusive extreme and allegory representing the most obtrusive, and each category overlapping somewhat with its neighbor. Nor is this to suggest that one form of symbolic communication is necessarily superior to another, for there are instances of good and inept uses of all these techniques.

Motifs are so totally integrated within the realistic texture of a film that we can almost refer to them as "submerged" or "closet" symbols. A *motif* can be a technique, an object — anything that's repeated systematically yet doesn't call attention to itself. Even after repeated viewings of a film, a *motif* is not always apparent, for its symbolic significance is never permitted to emerge or "detach" itself from its literalness. The repetition of circular or eye-shaped objects in *Psycho* is a good example of a *motif* in film, as we shall see.

Symbolism, on the other hand, comes out of the closet eventually. Like *motifs,* symbols can be palpable "things," but these things progressively acquire more abstract and general meanings in a given context, and these additional meanings are relatively apparent. Only a naive viewer can look upon "Rosebud," for example, as merely a snow-sled at the conclusion of *Citizen Kane*.

Metaphors, as we have seen, are even more obtrusive than symbols, for it is difficult not to notice the stylisation and self-consciousness of metaphoric statements in film.

Allegory is the most highly obtrusive symbolic element in film, for there is little likelihood of interpreting allegory literally (figs. 20, 21). In

FIG. 20. *Weekend* (1967), directed by Jean-Luc Godard. Sometimes there is a thin line dividing symbolism from allegory in film. One of the distinctions is the rather obtrusive theatricality of allegory, its high degree of stylisation, such as the colossal auto wrecks in Godard's film.

FIG. 21. *Weekend*. Godard's apocalyptic allegory of contemporary life features many whimsical digressions, such as the protagonists' meeting with "Emily Bronte" (above) and "Tom Thumb" in an "enchanted wood."

Bergman's *The Seventh Seal (Det sjunde inseglet),* for example, there's not much doubt in anyone's mind about what the character Death "represents."

Most film critics tend to concentrate on the middle ranges of this spectrum. Allegory, after all, is rather self-evident, and the significance of *motifs* often goes totally unperceived. But this critical concentration on symbolism at the expense of *motifs*, metaphors and allegory has resulted in an unfortunate one-sidedness. For example, a film like Hitchcock's *Psycho*—which employs *motifs* with great richness and frequency—is not treated with the same critical seriousness as a work like Fellini's *La Strada,* which is more overtly symbolic. At the other end of the spectrum, films employing radical metaphors and allegorical elements are often considered incoherent or self-indulgent. The works of Godard, for example, are frequently dismissed on these grounds, and a movie like *Persona* is generally considered inferior to Bergman's more conventionally symbolic works, like *Wild Strawberries (Smultronstället).*

Psycho and *Persona* are both masterpieces, though in different ways. Both movies have been explicated in elaborate detail. John Simon's lengthy analysis of *Persona*[7] is a first-rate piece of criticism, and the ubiquitous Robin Wood has discussed both films with predictable incisiveness.[8] Aside from the fact that each of these works deals with the subject of schizophrenia, there's little else they have in common. Like most of Hitchcock's works, *Psycho* is totally accessible to mass audiences: it's a "commercial thriller," which can be enjoyed on that level alone. But the film is also deeply philosophical, exploring metaphysical ideas primarily through its complex texture of *motifs*. *Persona,* on the other hand, is self-consciously an "art film." Like Hitchcock's movie, it tells a story, but its narrative development is not likely to appeal to general audiences. Indeed, even "art house" patrons tend to be put off by its complex metaphorical techniques, and rather than trying to understand how these techniques work, many viewers simply dismiss the film as "obscure" and "self-indulgent."

There are a number of *motif* patterns in *Psycho,* but the most important deals with the idea of eyes and circular shapes which tend to suggest eyes. Most audiences are not likely to notice this pattern on first viewing, for Hitchcock's plot is so absorbing that it compels virtually all of the viewer's attention. Even after repeated exposure,

---

7. *Ingmar Bergman Directs* (New York: Harcourt Brace Jovanovich, Inc., 1972).
8. *Ingmar Bergman* (New York: Praeger. 1969), and *Hitchcock's Films* (New York: A. S. Barnes & Co., 1969, Second Enlarged Edition).

this *motif* doesn't call attention to itself, for the shots are so cunningly integrated into the texture of the narrative, they might easily be interpreted as "atmospheric" details. But Hitchcock is one of the most supremely self-conscious film directors in cinematic history. He prides himself on never wasting a shot, and has spoken of the agonising decisions concerning just where to use a specific shot. Furthermore, Hitchcock's shooting scripts are meticulously detailed—often including frame drawings for every shot—and he disdains the very idea of improvising on a set. Everything is in the script before he begins shooting. The actual filming, according to him, is "merely a technical matter." If *Psycho* had been directed by anyone else, we might be inclined to believe that the elaborate eye *motif* in the film was merely a series of fortuitous accidents. With Hitchcock, however, such a view is unthinkable: he's too calculating, too precise an artist.

The movie opens with an extreme long shot of Phoenix, Arizona. The camera slowly cranes in toward a hotel and finally enters the dark window of a room where two illicit lovers, Marion Crane (Janet Leigh) and Sam Loomis (John Gavin) are putting on their clothes. The theme of voyeurism is immediately established: the "eye" of the camera (and the audience) has entered the shuttered "eye" of the hotel room. The film deals with the theme of sexual frustration and the sublimation of "normal" sex urges into perverse channels. In keeping with this theme, Hitchcock's opening shot can be interpreted as a kind of phallic thrust: the camera's penetration of the window can be viewed as a sublimation of our sexual as well as voyeuristic impulses, for indeed the two are closely related throughout the film.

Marion wants to marry Sam, but without money (most of his income goes toward alimony payments) he believes that their marriage would be doomed to failure. Impulsively, the desperate Marion steals $40,000 from her employer and flees to Sam's modest home in California. On the road she is stopped by a suspicious policeman, whose sunglasses are particularly threatening because they prevent her (and us) from seeing his eyes. A storms begins and to the increasingly paranoiac Marion the glaring headlights of the oncoming cars seem like accusing eyes. The downpour intensifies, and Marion's windshield wipers slash furiously back and forth, an audio-visual forshadowing of her death later in the film. Inadvertently, she leaves the main highway and stops eventually at the gloomy Bates Motel, where the boyish proprietor, Norman Bates (Anthony Perkins), asks her if she would like to share his modest supper before resting for the night.

A secondary *motif* in the film deals with the idea of "doubles," or the split personality. In many of Hitchcock's movies, the protagonist is split into two people, either figuratively, as in *Strangers on a Train,* or literally, as in *Vertigo*. In *Psycho,* this doubles *motif* is more complex, for we have a number of figurative split personalities (Marion, Sam, and the detective Arbogast) and an acutal schizophrenic (Norman) whose personality merges ultimately with his dead mother's. Hitchcock suggests this doubling in part through his use of mirror shots. When Marion lies to Norman about her name and address, for example, we see her and her reflected image in a mirror. Reflected images are also exploited in shots of Sam, Arbogast, and especially Norman.

Another secondary *motif* concerns the idea of immobility, which is associated with stillness, catatonic withdrawal, and death. In Norman's back parlor, we see a number of stuffed birds looming ominously on the walls. He tells Marion that "stuffing things" is his hobby. The two warm up to each other instinctively. He tells her of his sharp-tongued invalid mother, who is mentally ill. In discussing the terrible demands Mrs. Bates makes on her lonely son, Norman stresses that she is not a raving lunatic. Thoughtfully, Marion replies that perhaps "we all go a little mad sometimes," obviously referring to her rash theft of the $40,000. Moved by her conversation with Norman, she silently resolves to return to Phoenix, her "private trap," and accept her punishment. They say good night, and she returns to her room.

Inside the room, Marion tallies what she'll owe her employer when she returns to Phoenix. She tears up the paper with her calculations and flushes the scraps down the circular toilet, which Hitchcock shows us in a close shot. In the adjoining office, Norman removes a picture from the wall, revealing a circular shaped peephole. Literalising his voyeur *motif,* Hitchcock offers us a close shot of Norman peering into the hole, then an extreme close-up of Norman's eye. We are also given a point-of-view shot through the circular hole, showing us Marion disrobing for her shower. Hitchcock forces us to become voyeurs along with Norman, thus encouraging a sense of complicity with the youth, and forcing us to share his sexual guilt.

The celebrated shower sequence is where the circle-eye *motif* becomes most apparent. Hitchcock intercuts shots of the round shower head with close-ups of Marion's relieved face. The pouring water, with its symbolic implications of the cleansing of guilt, is subtly counterpointed by a slight thumping sound, reminiscent of the slashing wiper blades of the earlier drive through the storm. Silhouetted through the shower curtain, the form of a woman holding up a knife suddenly appears. While the soundtrack throbs with birdlike shrieks, Marion is brutally slashed by the knife-weilding assailant.

In a brilliantly-edited sequence, we see shots of Marion's mutilated body being struck again and again. Included in this sequence are close-ups of Marion's open mouth and shots of the circular bathtub drain, swirling furiously with water and blood. This image in turn dissolves to a parallel shot of an open eye, which seems immobilised in terror. Slowly, the camera begins to withdraw, and we realise that Marion's eye has not even blinked. As the camera continues to pull back, we see that the young woman's face is grotesquely pressed against the floor, yet we are unwilling to believe that the protagonist has died mid-way through the film. The camera continues its inexorable retreat, and Marion's features remain immobile. Hitchcock "vignettes" the edges of his shot, thus reinforcing his circular *motif* and suggesting that we are still looking through a kind of peephole. The undeniable eroticism of the shower scene is subtly underscored by the camera's slow withdrawal at the end of this sequence: the movement back is also a reversal of the opening shot of the film, suggesting a kind of phallic withdrawal. The fusing of the drain image with that of the eye suggests that behind both "openings" lies a sewer of some kind, one literal, another spiritual.

When Norman discovers the body, he is appalled at his "mother's" crime. He washes up the bathroom, then his own bloodied hands in a circular sink: again we see the blood swirling down the drain. Norman then piles the corpse and Marion's belongings into her car, and submerges all of this guilty evidence in a nearby swamp. When the sinking car seems to become momentarily stuck, the white roof of the auto almost resembles a huge eye peering up from the black mire of the swamp.

Eventually, Marion's sister Lila (Vera Miles) comes in pursuit of the fugitive. Sam, shocked that Marion would be capable of such a crime (her "double," Lila, seems unsurprised), agrees to help the sister in her search. In time, they find their way to the Bates Motel. While Sam detains Norman in the motel office, Lila goes up to the nearby house to question Mrs. Bates about the disappearance of Marion. Previously, we saw Norman carrying his mother to the fruit cellar in the basement of the house, where presumably she is still hiding. As Lila searches the upstairs bedrooms, Hitchcock stretches the suspense by cross-cutting to the motel office, where Norman is growing increasingly suspicious of Sam's probing. Among the objects in Mrs. Bates's bedroom is a strange sculpture of a pair of hands, eerily truncated and immobilised in bronze. Hitchcock also offers a shot of Mrs. Bates's circular sink, recalling parallel shots of the sink and toilet in the motel bathroom.

Eventually Lila finds her way to the cellar, where she sees Mrs. Bates from behind, seated on a swivel chair. Hitchcock treats this scene ironically and with characteristically ghoulish humor. With triumphant mockery, he even includes a glaring lightbulb within the frame, for the Ultimate Revelation ought to be accompanied by much light. Lila calls the old woman, but gets no response. To prolong the suspense, Hitchcock uses a point-of-view dolly, representing Lila's movement towards Mrs. Bates. Just before the moment of truth, we see a reverse angle shot of Lila, the circular lightbulb dominating the frame. When she turns the chair around, we see a hideously grinning skeleton under a cheap department store wig. Recoiling in horror, Lila hits the light-bulb, sending it spinning wildly, thus plunging the sockets of the skeleton's eyes into alternating pools of blackness and light. From behind Lila, Norman suddenly charges into the room, wrapped in his mother's disheveled clothing, the murder knife poise to strike. The soundtrack again resounds with bird-like screeches, but just as Norman is about to stab the girl, Sam comes from behind and subdues the killer.

The next scene takes place in the police station, where a smug psychiatrist "explains" the events of the story with unctuous confidence. (Psychiatrists and policemen are usually satirised for their complacency in Hitchcock's films, for they are seldom there when they're really needed.) He tells Lila and Sam that he learned of Norman's story from Mrs. Bates. Ten years earlier, in a fit of passionate jealousy, the boy murdered his mother and her illicit lover. Unable to withstand his guilt, Norman "shared" his personality with his mother, even to the point of trying to preserve her corpse by "stuffing" it, and by dressing up in her clothing on occasion. But eventually his part of this split personality was absorbed by the stronger half of Mrs. Bates. Hitchcock then cuts to a shot of Norman in his prison cell which is deathly still. We are reminded of Norman's statement to Marion about the "cruel eyes" that would stare at his mother if he should put her away in a mental institution. Now it is we who stare at Norman/Mrs. Bates. On the soundtrack we hear the voice of Mrs. Bates. She totally repudiates the crimes of her "dead" son, and even refuses to move, lest "they" think her guilty. Norman/Mrs. Bates has withdrawn into complete catatonic immobility. In order to "prove" her innocence, she will not even move her hand to swat a fly for she suspects that she is being watched.

Hitchcock concludes his film with a triple exposure shot that is so subtle many viewers miss it. Norman/Mrs. Bates looks up at the camera —at us—with a knowing smile of complicity. For a brief instant, this face merges with an image of Mrs. Bates' skull, which simultaneously dissolves to an image of Marion's submerged car being dredged from the swamp. This fleeting multiple-exposure shot is perhaps the most conspicuous metaphor of the film, fusing the *motifs* of eyes, immobility, and submerged guilt into a single image of overpowering force. The chain pulling up the car almost seems attached to Norman's heart, suggesting that his internal guilt as well as the auto is being dredged up to the light of exposure. Appropriately, the movie ends with this car shot, for it's a comprehensive symbol of the secret guilt which is shared by so many of the other characters—and so many of us in the audience also. The withdrawal *motif* of this shot also serves as the final reversal of the film's opening image of penetration.

Throughout the film, Hitchcock exploits the emotional associations of ordinary objects in so subtle a manner that the symbolic implications of these objects seem to function almost on a subliminal level. Unlike most symbols in movies, we seldom recognise the double function of Hitchcock's *motifs* while we're actually watching the film. But close scrutiny of these details is well worth the effort, for the director fuses the *motifs* of windows, eyes, drains, and sewers into a subtext of such astonishing complexity, and a vision of such profound pessimism, that Robin Wood's description of the film as a "descent into hell" seems scarcely strong enough.

Like Hitchcock's film, *Persona* is thematically too elaborate to be discussed at length here. Indeed, in terms of form, Bergman's film is one of the most complex movies ever made, in large part because of its dense metaphorical texture. Within this one work, the director uses virtually every kind of cinematic metaphor: editing tropes as well as aural, kinetic, and optical metaphors. There are also a great many *motifs* in *Persona*, including some of the same that are found in *Psycho*: the "doubles" motif, images of immobility, blood, hands, and eyes. Like *Psycho*, Bergman's film deals with the idea of schizophrenia, both on a psychological level and as a symbolic basis for more philosophical and metaphysical concerns.

The major plot line of Bergman's film is less complicated than Hitchcock's. A well known actress, Elisabet Volger (Liv Ullmann) suddenly stops speaking while perfoming on the stage in the title role of *Electra*. After many days of total silence, when she refuses to talk even to her husband and young son, she is referred to a psychiatric hospital. Alma (Bibi Andersson) an impressionable young nurse, is asked to take charge of the actress at the summer cottage of the psychiatrist, where the doctor hopes that the young nurse might induce the actress to speak. Alone on the rocky island, the two women are drawn together emotionally, though Elisabet continues to remain silent. Encourgaged by Elisabet's flattering attention and affection, Alma painfully recounts a story of an orgy in which she once took part. As a result, the nurse became pregnant and eventually decided to have an abortion. In telling the story, Alma only now begins to feel the anguish and guilt of her past acts. After this shared confidence, the nurse is drawn to Elisabet more than ever, even to the point of imagining that the two are very much alike, both physically and temperamentally.

All this while, the mysterious Elisabet listens attentively, sometimes with compassion, at other times with a certain affectionate amusement. Alma's life seems so trivial in comparison with the horrors that Elisabet has apparently experienced. When Alma offers to mail her patient's letter, the nurse is unable to resist the temptation to read it, for Elisabet has neglected to seal the envelope. In her letter, the actress writes with detached curiosity of Alma's sexual experiences. Elisabet cannot resist "studying" her friend. (Possibly for a future role?) This casual betrayal has a traumatic effect on Alma. From this point in the film, we're never sure whether we are watching real events or imagined ones. Nor are we certain whether the fantasist is Alma or Elisabet—though most likely it is Alma. The two women quarrel violently. Their identities begin to merge, subtly at first, then dramatically, uncontrollably. Alma even makes love with Mr. Vogler, while Elisabet watches with detachment, sorrow, and hopelessness. Bergman includes a number of other fantasy sequences between the two women which take place in a kind of timeless void. Alma tries desperately to resist merging personalities with Elisabet, but is unsuccessful. Suddenly, Elisabet mysteriously disappears. Soon after, we see Alma packing her clothes, shutting up the cottage, and departing alone on an empty bus. The psychiatric story ends here—with an unresolved, ambiguous conclusion.

Despite its enormous dramatic power, this is only the narrative scaffolding of Bergman's film, for the movie is also an elaborate philosophical exploration of the problems and responsibilities of the artist in relationship to his political and social environment. The story of the two women is enclosed by a kind of frame, which consists of a series of brief, almost subliminal shots. Many of these shots are not contextually related to the story proper, but serve as metaphors for Bergman's philosophical themes. These editing tropes are found not only at the beginning and ending of the film, but also at the mid-point, where they erupt violently as Alma's love for Elisabet turns to hatred.

The elaborate pre-credit and credit sequence functions almost like a musical overture, briefly introducing most of the important ideas that will be developed in the story proper. Some of the shots in this sequence defy precise analysis, and even Bergman is unsure of what a few of them mean. At this point in viewing the film we are not expected to know the significance of most of these shots. They function mostly on a visceral level to jolt us from our passivity.

The opening shot of the film shows us the carbon arc lamps of a movie projector lighting up. Then, in quick succession, we see a film strip unfurling off the sprockets of a projector, and some movie images whirling out of control on a screen. Bergman then cuts to a shot of an inverted cartoon figure washing her face in the water of a rocky banked harbor. The sprocket holes of this animated film can be seen plainly. All of these images suggest that *Persona* will deal at least in part with the problems of making movies, perhaps that the figures of Alma and Elisabet are themselves personas or masks for Bergman's own artistic and psychological experiences. The mechanical breakdown of the projector certainly suggests a metaphorical forshadowing of the breakdown of the emotional mechanisms of the two women.

The shot of the animated woman washing is followed by a close-up of two real hands washing. Robin Wood interprets this juxtaposition as a comment on the pitiful ineffectuality of art in capturing real experiences, that art—no matter how complex—must always seem a ludicrously inadequate caricature of the real thing. John Simon sees the juxaposition as an indication of the various styles and points of view that Bergman will use throughout the film. Bergman then cuts to a fast motion sequence which seems to be an old silent movie farce, with a man being pursued by the devil and a skeleton. Again, one is tempted to view this scene as a tacit comment on the inadequacies of film art in dealing with such complex themes as death and evil.

The director then intercuts three shots that suggest religious ideas. First, there is a shot of a black spider, which seems to be an allusion to Bergman's earlier *Through a Glass Darkly (Såysom i en spegel)*. (In that film, an artist—in this case, a novelist—is fascinated by his own daughter's descent into madness, and is using her experiences as a basis for his creativity. At the end of the film, the girl imagines that she sees God—a terrifying black spider.) The second shot is an overexposed image of a dead lamb being slashed open. A hand reaches into its belly and dredges out its bowels. The camera pans slightly, and we see the lamb's glassy eye staring dumbly . The third shot of this brief sequence shows a spike being driven into a hand, an obvious crucifixion allusion. It is difficult to know whether Bergman is suggesting the Christ-like agony of the artist in creating, or the agony of his "victims," his subject-matter from real life. Perhaps both ideas are implied, for in the story proper both Elisabet (the artist figure) and Alma (the "raw material" of art) undergo terrible anguish.

Bergman then offers a shot of a blank concrete wall, which dissolves to a shot of some trees, stripped of their foliage, in a bleak winter setting. Next, we see an image of a spiked iron fence, with a bank of snow in front of it. This in turn leads to a series of close shots of an old woman lying silently in what seems to be a hospital—or perhaps a morgue, for one shot is a close-up of her hand hanging lifelessly off the edge of the bed. On the soundtrack, we hear some eerie dripping sounds, metaphors perhaps for the passage of time, or dripping drops of blood, life's basic substance.

Bergman then begins one of the most ambiguous series of shots in this pre-credit sequence. We see a pubescent boy lying naked under a white sheet. Unable to sleep, the boy sits up, puts on his glasses and tries to read, but he is too restless. He then looks at the camera—at us—and his hand gropes slowly towards the lens. The movement seems to suggest a reaching out, but also a kind of conjuring effect. Bergman then gives us a reverse angle shot, and we see that the boy is reaching toward an out-of-focus image of a woman's face—in fact an alternating image of Bibi Andersson and Liv Ullmann. This sequence has been interpreted in various ways, but Bergman deliberately keeps its symbolism ambiguous. The boy could represent Elisabet's son, whom she has guiltily rejected. He could also be an embodiment of Alma's aborted child: his groping for her face could represent Alma's subjective projection of guilt. But the boy is also a kind of conjurer of images, and as such, he could represent Bergman himself, child-like before his own creations which seem to overpower him.

At this point the credits begin, but interspersed with them are various shots that are actually a continuation of the pre-credit sequence. Included is an image of Liv Ullmann as Elisabet playing Electra. There is also a shot of a barren rocky sea-coast, which will be the major setting of the story proper, and a television image of a Buddhist monk immolating himself. There is also an extreme close-up of a pair of lips, only photographed vertically, so that the image almost seems to resemble a vagina. Possibly the shot is meant to suggest the idea of giving birth: George Bernard Shaw, as well as Freud, believed that the artist is essentially a neurotic, who, in creating a work of art, is subconsciously trying to mimic a woman's giving birth "normally." The fact that this image appears at the "birth" of the film tends to confirm this interpretation.

Bergman then intercuts three close-ups with his concluding titles. The boy's close-up is repeated a number of times. We then are offered a shot of Alma and one of Elisabet, both of them, like the boy, staring directly into the camera. The two women are photographed in such a way that their striking physical resemblance is emphasised. The fact that these three shots are so conspicuously parallel seems to suggest that they all represent aspects of the same single consciousness.

All of these sequences take no longer than a few minutes of screen time. The story proper begins with the psychiatrist recounting Elisabet's breakdown to Alma. The fact that the actress began to giggle while playing Electra is significant. *Electra* deals with the theme of matricide, of a child's revenge for a mother's betrayal. We later learn that Elisabet hated being a mother because it interfered with her artistic career. The complex pattern of guilt this hatred produced in Elisabet is apparently what precipitated her giggles and later silent withdrawal. Art seems so *simple* in comparison with life. Later, in the hospital room, Elisabet again begins to giggle when she hears a radio melodrama which strikes her as a ludicrous caricature of real-life counterparts.

Bergman never offers us an explicit explanation for Elisabet's withdrawal, but by permitting us to watch Alma's step-by-step withdrawal, we can infer the causes underlying the actress's condition, for they are virtually the same: the betrayals, compromises, deceptions, and self-deceptions of everyday life are what destroy both women. In a powerful scene which is photographed in a very long take, Bergman gives us a close-up of Elisabet lying in bed in the hospital. Slowly, very slowly, her face is gradually submerged into total darkness.

Another hospital scene tends to confirm this interpretation of Elisabet as a despairing artist figure. The actress is watching television, where she sees a newsreel of the war in Vietnam. Suddenly the TV screen is filled with a shot of a Buddhist monk setting fire to himself in protest. Elisabet recoils in horror, withdrawing to a corner of the room—the very edge of Bergman's frame. In a series of shots that cut closer and closer to Elisabet's face we see all the anguish and despair that has precipitated her revolt of silence. But no matter how much she withdraws, the horrors of reality are always there—even if at second hand, on a TV screen.

Once the scene shifts to the island retreat, Elisabet's condition seems to improve, though Bergman often cuts to shots of the barren rocks which act as constant reminders of the essential sterility of such an isolated existence. As the women draw closer, Bergman photographs them in complementary costumes, parallel set-ups, and even blocks their movements so that their bodies seem to merge. This "double" *motif* is carried over into a dream sequence (probably Alma's) where Elisabet enters the nurse's room through one door and leaves through another parallel to it. Photographed mostly in slow motion and given a hazy effect, this graceful sequence is one of the first overt dramatisations of the merging of personalities. Both women stand before a dark mirror, where Elisabet pulls back Alma's hair to reveal their striking physical resemblance.

Like Hitchcock, Bergman acknowledges the audience in his film. Lest we become too complacent in viewing this "freak show," the director begins one sequence with a shot of the rocky shore. Suddenly, from beneath the frame, Elisabet emerges with a still camera and clicks our picture. Like *Psycho, Persona* is as much a portrait of ourselves as it is a study of the "neurotic" characters of the film.

Roughly at the mid-point of the movie, Alma learns of Elisabet's betrayal. After reading the letter, the nurse stands thoughtfully at the edge of the water, in a shot which emphasises the "doubles" *motif* by including her full reflection. Seething with repressed anger, Alma leaves a jagged piece of glass on the walkway, where she hopes Elisabet will pass. When she does, Bergman cuts to a shot of Alma looking at the scene from behind a window and curtain. Suddenly the soundtrack reverberates with a cracking noise, and the image splits down the middle. Half the image drops from sight, literally splitting Alma's face into two. This "crack up" is a metaphor of Alma's emotional collapse. A burning hole then penetrates Alma's face and consumes the image surface. Beneath the burn hole, incongruous images of the pre-credit silent movie devil and the skeleton emerge—Bergman's reminders of the primitiveness and inadequacies of his medium in conveying intense passions.

After the two women quarrel, Alma withdraws to the rocks where she remains for hours, silently huddled in an immobile trance. In her bedroom, Elisabet finds a photograph of a Nazi concentration camp and its victims. Again, she is struck by the horrors of the real world, particularly by a small Jewish boy who is among those being herded. The boy perhaps recalls her own son, whom we saw earlier in a photograph. The fact that Elisabet is jolted back to reality by several "documentary" images reflects, perhaps, Bergman's own despair in trying to capture honest and uncompromised emotions in a "fictional" image.

After this, we are never sure whether what we are seeing are fantasies or events that actually take place. In one particularly dream-like sequence, Elisabet's husband (who is apparently blind) visits the cottage. Mr. Vogler speaks to Alma as though she were his wife. At first, Alma resists, but prodded by the mysterious Elisabet, Alma pretends to be his wife, even going so far as to make love with him, while the silent Elisabet seems to recall her marital relationship with sorrow and futility.

In another sequence, Alma sees Elisabet guiltily covering the torn photograph of her son with her hands. The nurse prods the mother to speak of her boy, but Elisabet refuses. Instead, Alma tells the story, almost as though it were her own. As she recounts Elisabet's horror at being pregnant and in giving birth to an unwanted child, the camera moves from an over-the-shoulder two-shot to a close-up of Elisabet — half her face plunged in darkness. Then Bergman repeats the same story of guilt and anguish, only this time he moves the camera towards Alma, the opposite side of her face likewise in darkness. The repetition of the story with the two separate shots suggests the merging of personalities. Alma denies this identity fusion, but suddenly, through the use of special effects photography, Bergman literally fuses the faces of the two women into one.

Near the end of the film, we see Elisabet packing her clothes. Later, we see Alma doing the same. She looks into a mirror, and again we see an image of fused identities, dreamily shot in double-exposure. As Alma leaves the cottage with her suitcase, Bergman crowds her figure with the wooden face of a ship's masthead. He then cuts to a close-up of Elisabet's immobile features as Electra, which is strikingly similar. This in turn is intercut with a shot of Bergman and his cinematographer Sven Nykvist behind a camera, which is descending slowly on a crane. The juxtaposition of these three shots once again suggests their parallelism, implying that Alma and Elisabet are two sides of Bergman's own personality.

The film concludes with a reversal of some of the opening shots. We see the boy reaching for a totally out-of-focus image of the Andersson/Ullmann face. The soundtrack seems to whirl out of control, as we see an image of the film strip uncoiling wildly off its sprocket. Finally, the carbon arc lamps of the projector fade and there is only darkness.

Even a casual examination of *Persona* alone would flatly contradict the statements of those literary gentlemen who for years have been claiming that metaphor is difficult if not impossible to produce in the cinema. There are many other generalisations that have been made about film and literature that are equally open to question: that film has only one tense, the present; that movies must be more simple than literature because they are a mass medium (as though printing were not); that films cannot deal with conceptual ideas; that language must be less complex in film than in literature. And so on. A re-examination of these critical canards is long overdue.

4
Alice's Restaurant and the Tradition of the Plotless Film

The Americans, who are much more stupid when it's a question of analysis, instinctively succeed in constructing things.
—Jean-Luc Godard

We're into another way of looking at narrative now. We've got to be willing to abandon a straight narrative line in terms of circular, cyclical narrative. The old style is not sufficient. We can't go in quest of just another story. . . . The repetitive characteristics of patterns of living have affected direct narrative so that seemingly disconnected events become meaningful.
—Arthur Penn

I

The genius of American films, according to Godard, is in their narrative structures, their plots. Most critics would agree, particularly Europeans, who have consistently admired the American cinema for its narrative vitality. Griffith, Chaplin, Ford, Hitchcock, Welles — they're all great story-tellers. Indeed, most of the giants of the American cinema have worked best in *genre* films, those movies—slapstick comedy, thrillers, westerns, melodrama—that emphasise plot above all.

The term "plot" is hard to define in an absolute sense. Even a movie like Antonioni's *Zabriskie Point*—which most people would agree is "plotless"—has *some* narrative elements. The word is best used in a relative sense, implying a degree of emphasis, just as in fiction and drama, one would refer to Fielding's *Tom Jones* and Sophocles' *Oedipus the King* as "tightly plotted," and Proust's *Remembrance of Things Past* and Chekhov's *Three Sisters* as relatively "plotless." This is certainly not to suggest, of course, that weakly plotted works are inferior in any way: only different. There is also a difference between "structure" and "plot" which ought to be preserved here. The structure of a work of art can refer to *any* arrangement of inter-related units to a complex single entity. The structure of a film refers to its principle of coherence—how the parts relate to the whole. The plot of a movie, on the other hand, is merely one *kind* of structure, one emphasising events, and the causal inter-relationships of events.

Like the majority of plays, most American films tend to be structured along a straight line of consecutive inter-related events. A specific problem or conflict is introduced in the exposition. This conflict is systematically intensified until it reaches a climax, at which point the conflict is resolved one way or the other. The key word here is "systematically." There is a kind of logic or inevitability that most strongly-plotted works possess. Usually this logic depends upon a strict sense of causality, with an emphasis on the *consequences* of acts.

In a play, each scene progressively intensifies the conflict in an ascending pattern, accelerating the problem toward an inevitable climax. In a tightly-plotted movie, this sense of inevitability is even more intense, for virtually every shot is directed toward this end. With a plotless work (whether a novel, play, or film), one could rearrange the sequence of many (though usually not all) scenes with relatively little loss of comprehension. For example, except for the first and last volumes, the separate "books" of *Remembrance of Things Past* need not be read "in sequence," for in effect Proust denies the validity of chronological time and sequential action as meaningful methods of organising experience. Similarly, in *Last Year at Marienbad (L'année dernière à Marienbad)*, Alain Resnais totally destroys the concept of linear time. The shots from this film could be re-edited without much significant alteration in the "cause/effect pattern," for Resnais deliberately frustrates our attempts to force the scenes into a linear style. To scramble the sequence of events in a tightly-plotted work, however, would result in chaos: nothing would "make sense," for the cause effect continuity would be destroyed. Re-editing *Psycho* would produce only a meaningless jumble, for Hitchcock never wastes a shot, and every shot in this movie is precisely calculated to fit into a cunning linear progression—even while he is satirising the very absurdity of "logic" and "reasonable explanations."

Strongly plotted movies tend to use details sparingly: like a "well-made play" they are seldom offered for their own sake, but contribute directly to the narrative development. When a detail seems gratuitous, or doesn't seem to "fit," we can usually be sure that it will re-emerge significantly later in the narrative. The future, then, is extremely important in a strongly-plotted movie: everything in the present is directed toward that "obligatory scene" which will occur late in the film. For this reason most audiences have a "sense" of a film's ending. They can anticipate it without much difficulty, for all the previous shots and scenes have been manipulated in such a way as to direct the audience's expectations toward that climactic confrontation in the future when "the problem" will be solved.

Most film directors who have discarded or de-emphasised plots have done so on the grounds that they are too contrived, too artificial and calculating. Almost invariably, such artists claim that narrative structures are unrealistic, untrue to the way things happen in real life. Some film-makers (particularly those emphasising the freedom of the will) dislike the sense of Destiny or Fate that plots tend to suggest. In *Feeling and Form* Susanne Langer refers to the dramatic mode as the "Mode of Destiny." Though she speaks only of the plots to plays, her remarks are equally relevant to films that emphasise narrative structures:

> Dramatic action is a semblance of action so constructed that a whole indivisible piece of virtual history is implicit in it, as a yet unrealized form, long before the presentation is completed. . . . It is a human destiny that unfolds before us, its unity is apparent from the opening words, or even silent action, because on the stage we see acts in their entirety, as we do not see them in the real world except in retrospect, that is, by constructive reflection. . . . Stage action is not, like genuine action, embedded in a welter of irrelevant doings and divided interests. . . . We can view each smallest act in its context, as a symptom of character and condition. We do not have to find what is significant; the selection has been made—whatever is there is significant, and it is not too much to be surveyed *in toto*. A character stands before us as a coherent whole. It is with characters as with their situations: both become visable on the stage, transparent and complete as their analogues in the world are not.[1]

---

1. A selection of this book (entitled "The Dramatic Illusion") is reprinted in *Perspectives on Drama*, edited by James L. Calderwood and Harold E. Toliver (New York: Oxford University Press, 1968). The quoted passage in the text is taken from this anthology, pp. 254-55.

Though most plays conform to Mrs. Langer's description, a number of them do not. Wilder's *Our Town* and Thomas's *Under Milk Wood*, for example, seem rather random in their narrative organisation, and copious in details which are not always "significant" in her sense of the term. Furthermore, the post-Brechtian theater is considerably less manipulative than the traditional drama. Virtually all the Absurdist dramatists have attempted to destroy the tyrannies of "logic" and "significance," which are out-growths of the Aristotelian dramatic tradition.

Despite these important exceptions, Mrs. Langer's description of the nature of plots is a useful reverse springboard for a definition—or rather a general description—of "plotlessness" in films. Next to a deliberate de-emphasis of causality in the sequence of shots and scenes, perhaps the most characteristic quality of plotless movies is a general air of freedom and randomness: we can't predict how the characters will behave because certain telling clues have not been so rigorously pre-selected for us by the artist. Most plotless films offer many "irrelevant" details—that is, details which may not be "significant" (i.e., to the narrative), but are offered for their own sake either because of their innate charm or because they are palpably *there* on location, and contribute a certain authenticity. In short, the principles of selectivity often seem more arbitrary and subjective in plotless films than in plays and *genre* movies.

In the cinema, plotless works are more common than in the theater, perhaps because of the influence of the documentary (fig.1), which tends to be structured along principles other than narrative continuity. Most of the directors of these plotless films have readily admitted to being influenced by the "random" and aleatory charms of the documentary, most notably Jean Renoir, the Italian neo-realists, and Jean-Luc Godard.

In the United States, plotless films have seldom been successful with mass audiences. In the late Sixties and early Seventies, however, this form finally came into its own. With the enormous popularity of such essentially non-narrative movies as *Easy Rider* (fig. 2), *2001: A Space Odyssey*, *Medium Cool*, *Faces* (fig. 3), *Woodstock*, *Five Easy Pieces*, and *Alice's Restaurant*, one could almost claim that the plotless film became a dominant mode in American film-making, though the majority of movies made in the U.S.A. were (and still are) straightforward linear narratives.

Arthur Penn's *Alice's Restaurant* was perhaps the most impressive of this group of films. Penn, who has been called the "most European" of the younger American directors, seems to have been influenced by the work of Godard, who himself has been influenced by the documen-

FIG. 1. *The Musketeers of Pig Alley* (1912), directed by D. W. Griffith. Whenever possible, Griffith preferred to use actual locations rather than studio sets. Much of the "documentary" interest of this film was due to its lower East Side setting.

FIG. 2. *Easy Rider* (1969). directed by Dennis Hopper. Despite its rather melodramatic conclusion, this film was one of the few movies of this period that reflected the new youth culture with any degree of accuracy.

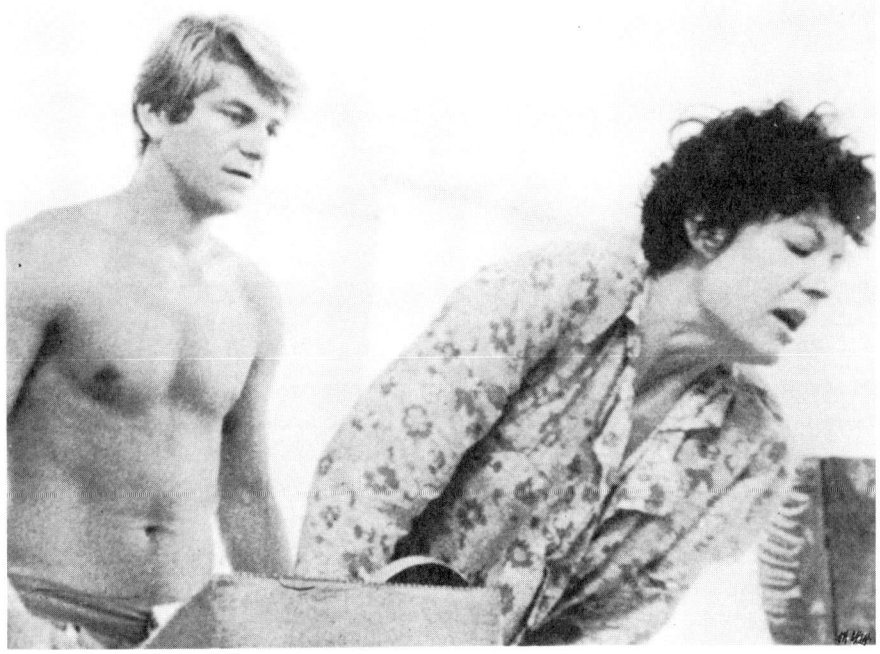

FIG. 3. *Faces* (1968), directed by John Cassavetes. Like his previous work *Shadows* (1960), Cassavetes's film was made on a small budget, used a number of non-professional actors, and had the look of a documentary rather than a fiction film.

tary tradition of the Italian neo-realists and the lyrical films of Jean Renoir. The history of the plotless film is — appropriately — unpredictable and even improbable, especially in its strange hybridisations.

II

From a strictly historical point of view, the plotless film can be dated almost to the inception of movies at the turn of the century. The earliest films of the Lumière brothers in France, for example, were not concerned with narrative but with capturing the variety and flux of everyday life. Anything that moved was fascinating for its own sake. Around 1900, movies portraying such events as the arrival of a train or a street parade were enormously popular. These short *actualités*, as they were sometimes called, constituted the first stage of what was later recognised as the documentary movement.

One of the major difficulties facing all documentarists involves the problem of structure. Without the aid of an articluated plot, the documentarist is plagued with having to unify a body of materials which often has no innate coherence. For short documentaries, the problem is minimal, for presumably the intrinsic interest of the materials will engross the viewer for the duration of the film. For feature-length movies, however, the problem is more acute, for audiences tend to grow restless when they are not presented with a story of some kind. American audiences are particularly addicted to plots, and not suprisingly, we have produced few documentarists of major stature in this country until recent times.

Robert Flaherty, an American documentarist of international repute, was not particularly successful with audiences after his first masterpiece, *Nanook of the North* (fig. 4). Significantly, all of Flaherty's movies are rather plotless, and all of them were more popular in Europe than in the United States. Perhaps the explanation for the popular success of *Nanook* with American audiences is to be found in its high adventure and romantic heroism. The life of the Eskimo Nanook and his family is more fraught with dangers than can be found in most conventional fiction films. Certainly it was not the plot that audiences responded to, for there is virtually none. Instead the movie is unified by three general movements or sections. The first takes place in the summer, when Nanook and his family have a brief period when they can enjoy the mild weather, and there is enough food for everyone. The second section deals at length with the harsh Arctic winter and the desperate fight for mere survival. The third section is even more intense, for it deals with a raging blizzard—the most ferocious of the year. Nanook and his family are almost destroyed by the storm, but their tenacious fortitude ultimately triumphs.

The climate and the constant quest for food form the structural spine of Flaherty's film, not a plot. Each season involves different preparations, each involves a kind of desperate outward expansion, for the seasons grow progressively harsher, and Nanook must search farther afield for food. Within each of the film's three movements, the shots could be rearranged without much loss of coherence. Indeed, in his later movies, Flaherty's footage was almost totally restructured by his often exasperated editors, simply because Flaherty himself lacked any narrative sense. He was far more concerned with the excitement of the immediate event, and seldom bothered very much about how the event would fit into an overall pattern.

Flaherty, however, is an aberration in American film-making. For the most part, our movies—until recently—have been tightly plotted, with an emphasis on events and the causal inter-relationships of events. We must look to France to trace the next major phase of the plotless film—to the lyrical masterpieces of Jean Renoir in the Thirties. Renior's movies were to exert a profound influence on the French New

FIG. 4. *Nanook of the North* (1921), directed by Robert Flaherty. Like the Eskimo ivory carvers, Flaherty liked to believe that his subjects were "found" rather than "created." He disliked imposing any structure on his materials, insisting that the structure was already there, waiting to be revealed by the camera.

Wave directors in the late Fifties and Sixties, particularly on François Truffaut, Agnès Varda, and Jean-Luc Godard.

Superficially, Renoir's movies seem to have little in common with those of Lumière and Flaherty. For one thing, the tone of their films is different: Renoir seems sensuous, intimate and relaxed whereas Lumiere is hard-nosed and factual, and Flaherty is grandly heroic. Furthermore, Renoir's films don't have that "educational" and didactic quality that pervades the documentary tradition. His movies ostensibly deal with fictional stories —albeit rather leisurely ones—whereas most documentaries are primarily concerned with revealing facts. But though Renoir's movies contain some plot elements, the narrative line seldom constitutes the major structural principle in his films of this period. Indeed, in *Une partie de campagne* (1936), there is no story as such, but merely a common setting which is used to bring together an interesting group of people (fig. 5). The film's structure seems more musical than narrative, for it is essentially a series of variations on a theme.

FIG. 5. *Picnic on the Grass* (1959), directed by Jean Renoir. Even by the late Fifties, Renoir tended to avoid excessively-plotted stories. In this film he returned to the variations-on-a-theme formula of the *Une partie de campagne*.

Alice's Restaurant *and the Tradition of the Plotless Film*

It's interesting to see how often Renoir used this variation-on-a-theme technique rather than plot to unify most of his movies of the Thirties. Sometimes a film might be centered around a character, like the irascible tramp in *Boudu Saved from Drowning (Boudu sauvé des eaux*, 1932), in which the variations consist of a number of people who are exploited or put down by Boudu. In *The Rules of the Game (La règle du jeu,* 1939), the country villa setting is the constant while the variations consist of an ever-shifting series of lovers and hangers-on (fig. 6). In *La grande illusion* (1937), Renoir explores the theme of captivity (fig. 7). The settings consist mostly of a sequence of German prisoner-of-war camps, but Renoir is interested in other kinds of imprisonment as well: the prisons of class, breeding, nationality, and religion.

In some respects, each of Renoir's variations on a theme can be looked upon as a kind of subplot, though this term generally implies a more systematic narrative development (however brief) than is generally the case with Renoir's variations. Whatever one wishes to call these relatively self-contained variations—sub-plots, digressions,

FIG. 6. *The Rules of the Game* (1939), directed by Jean Renoir. The mixing of *genres* is what often makes this film so unpredictable and disturbing, as in this scene where an adulterous philanderer is almost killed by a jealous husband in an elegant salon.

FIG. 7. *La grande illusion* (1937), directed by Jean Renoir. Renoir's techniques are so "simple" that their subtlety often goes unnoticed. The use of closed forms (tight framing, symmetrical compositions, stationary set-ups, the avoidance of pans, etc.) in this film is totally appropriate to the subject, which deals with the theme of imprisonment. Renoir uses open form techniques only when the men are free.

vignettes—they tend to weaken the narrative thrust of a work. If a movie is composed almost entirely of such variations, we can be reasonably sure that the film-maker is more concerned with a unifying theme, or a central idea, than with telling a story.

Renoir is essentially a lyric poet rather than a story-teller. The qualities we remember from his movies are their sensuousness, their warmth, and above all, their extraordinary charm. In most cases, their "plots" are forgotten—who can remember the *sequence* of scenes in these films, for example? (The sequence in a film like *Psycho*, on the other hand, is fairly easy to reconstruct, even for the casual moviegoer.) In short, these films have the same copiousness and open-endedness of life itself. Compared with most American movies, Renoir's works seem sprawling, even self-indulgent at times. There is none of the austerity, the economy of detail that characterises most

American films. Renoir's movies fairly spill over with a luxuriance of detail. As often as not, shots and even whole scenes are offered simply for their own sake—not because they "make a point" or further the plot (fig. 8).

In most of Renoir's films of this period, there is no sense of contrivance, of an artist pulling the strings. The extraordinary freshness of these movies—they have dated surprisingly little—is due in large part to their very plotlessness. There is an improvised air in many of these scenes—almost as though the director happened to pass by while the events were occuring in real life. This authenticity is further enhanced by the intermingling of genres: tragedy, comedy, pastoral are all jumbled together in a charmingly unpredictable manner. In short, our sense of *expectation*—an important element in plotted films—is often frustrated, through in a pleasing way.

Renoir's movies are often structured in terms of a series of parallels and polarities. These structural *motifs* are varied and juxtaposed in an intuitive rather than a progressively sequential manner. A favorite set of polarities—found in his films after the Thirties as well—involves the

FIG. 8. *La grande illusion*. The variations in this prisoner of war film consist of many types of imprisonment—of class, race, religion, and nationality.

idea of nature vs. civilisation (fig. 9). In *Boudu Saved from Drowning,* for example, the tramp Boudu is "rescued" from drowning in a river by a well-intentioned bourgeois bookshop owner. Throughout the film, Renoir is concerned with contrasting the two men in terms of life-styles and philosophical outlooks. The vital but disrupting tramp is associated with nature, especially water, trees, and the physical world in general. Like the animals of nature, he's amoral, impulsive, and "messy" in his instinctive disorderliness. Boudu is a man who satisfies the needs and pleasures of the body, without much concern for restraint, "good taste," and decorum, which are more typical of his benefactor-rescuer.

The bookseller is characterised by images of order, precision, intellectualism, and other ideas associated with bourgeois civilisation. His life centers around his bookshop, with its tidy categories of musty tomes and its confining walls. Even his mistress is employed within these walls. Renoir characteristically employs the image of a river — either literal, or flowing "rivers" of street and pedestrian traffic outside the shop—to emphasise Boudu's affinity to a life of constant

FIG. 9. *Picnic on the Grass.* As in many of Renoir's lyrical films, this one emphasises the polarities of civilization vs. nature, reason vs. impulse, order vs. anarchy.

Alice's Restaurant *and the Tradition of the Plotless Film* 145

change and renewal. The claustrophobic scenes which take place in the shop, on the other hand, symbolise the stagnation of "civilised" existence. Boudu is almost converted to this kind of life, but in the end he manages to escape while he and his bride are riding in a boat on a river. Boudu tips the boat over, floats down stream, then returns to his life of freedom, while his wife and friends believe him to be drowned. But the second "drowning" is actually a rebirth for him, a reconversion to his former pantheistic state of anarchy.

Despite the leisurely casualness of most of the scenes in the film, Renoir's movie is not carelessly constructed, for his is an art that conceals art. Indeed, without the advantages of a tight plot, Renoir was required to orchestrate his scenes with rigorous discipline, or he would have lost the interest of his audiences. As with many of the films of Truffaut, Renoir's cinematic disciple, the variety of styles and moods is unified by a persuasive conviction, the director's generosity and warmth. There are few villains in Renoir's movies, only weak misguided blunderers. "Every man has his reasons," he was fond of

FIG. 10. *Open City* (1945), directed by Roberto Rossellini. This seminal masterpiece featured the great Italian actress, Anna Magnani, and made her an international star.

saying—a paraphrase of the old French adage, "to understand is to forgive."

The Italian neo-realists immediately after the second World War combined many of the elements of both the documentary tradition and Renoir's lyrical tradition. Perhaps the most outstanding characteristic of neo-realism is its outright hostility toward plots. For this reason some critics assign the origin of the plotless fiction film to this period, since the Italians were explicit in their rejection—even to the point of issuing manifestos. The prototype of neo-realist movies, Roberto Rossellini's *Open City (Roma, città aperta,* 1945) quickly established a rallying point (fig. 10). There followed an extraordinary outburst of masterpieces: Vittorio De Sica's *Shoeshine (Sciuscià,* 1946), *Bicycle Thief (Ladri di bicicletti,* 1949), and *Umberto D* (1952); Luchino Visconti's *La terra trema* (1948); and Rossellini's *Paisan (Paisà,* 1946); not to speak of other less conspicuously brilliant movies by these and other directors.

Cesare Zavattini, who wrote the scripts to many of these films, also served as a publicist for the neo-realist movement. In a 1952 interview in *Sight and Sound*, Zavattini put forth what he felt were the major advantages of neo-realism over the tightly plotted films being produced in Hollywood:

> The most important characteristic, and the most important innovation, of what is called neo-realism, it seems to me, is to have realised that the necessity of the "story" was only an unconscious way of disguising a human defeat, and that the kind of imagination it involved was simply a technique of superimposing dead formulas over living social facts.[2]

Plots, according to Zavattini, have a way of pre-empting all of a director's screen time, permitting him only an occasional scene or two for what really concerns him—the "excavation" of facts, feelings, and ideas from everyday situations (fig. 11). Like most advocates of the plotless film, Zavattini insisted that narrative structures are untrue to the way things actually happen in life. The principles of selectivity are governed by the needs of a plot structure, rather than the desire to reflect accurately the limitless freedom of real life. Strongly emphasising the documentary "responsibilities" of the film-maker, Zavattini even suggests that the use of plots is a kind of moral evasion:

> While the cinema used to make one situation produce another situation,

---

2. "Some Ideas on the Cinema," reprinted in *Film: A Montage of Theories,* edited by Richard Dyer MacCann (New York: E. P. Dutton & Co., 1966), p. 217.

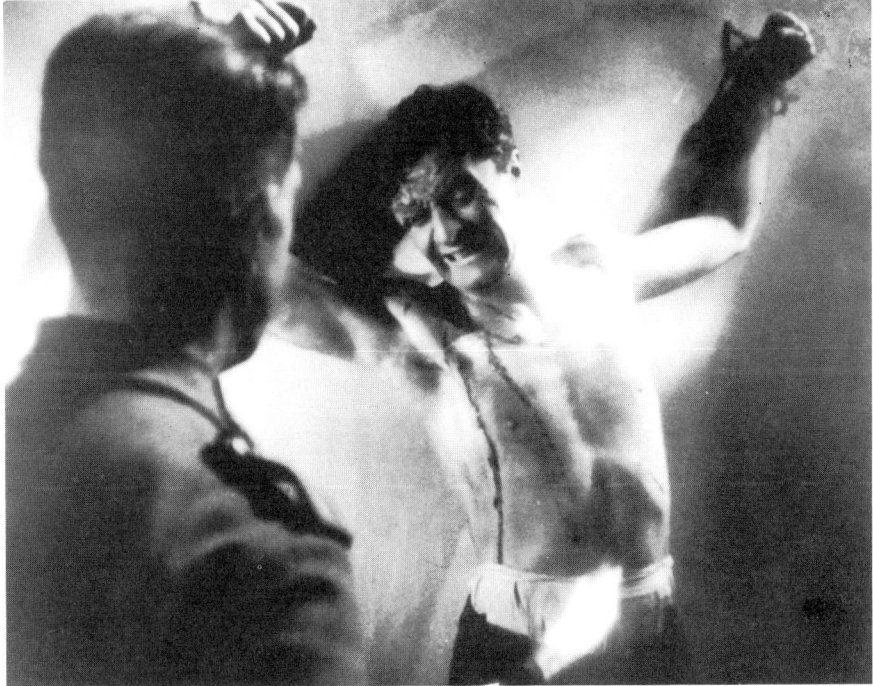

FIG. 11. *Open City*. Rossellini's film was a strange blend of Marxist and Christian existentialism. The Church and the Party are shown to be the two institutional pillars of the Italian Resistance.

and another, and another, again and again, and each scene was thought out and immediatedly related to the next (the natural result of a mistrust of reality), today when we have thought out a scene, we feel the need to "remain" in it, because the single scene itself can contain so many echoes and reverberations, can even contain all the situations we may need.[3]

Certain political considerations are relevant here, for among other things, neo-realism represented a Marxist reaction against Italian fascism. The neo-realists wanted to emphasise the moral freedom of individuals in dealing with oppressive institutions. In *Open City*, for example, Rossellini showed how some Italians actively fought against fascist authorities (fig. 12), while others passively accepted or even exploited their political domination. By showing a variety of possible political alternatives within an episodic and open structure, Rossellini implicitly emphasised the free choice open to all Italians. (The very title of the movie implies these existential ideas.) Nothing, Rossellini

3. *Ibid.*, pp. 218-19.

FIG. 12. *Open City*. Because good film stock was not available, Rossellini shot much of his film with inferior newsreel stock, yet the resultant gaminess enhanced the "documentary look" of his film.

suggests, is inevitable, nothing is unalterable. Human destiny is to a great extent a matter of self-determination. To convey these ideas in a tightly plotted structure is, in many ways, to be at odds with the essence of the ideas.

Besides emphasising freedom, multiplicity and alternative choices, most neo-realist movies also suggested a slice-of-life quality, with no clearly-defined beginning, middle and end (fig. 13). The inconclusive "conclusions" of these films bothered a great many American audiences at the time,for Americans were (any many still are) frustrated when problems are not solved in the final reel. Today inconclusive endings can be seen even in routine American movies of no particular artistic pretensions.

Neo-realism had an enormous influence on other film-producing nations. While some directors adhered to the old ways, many serious film-makers in Europe felt freed at last from the obligations of having to use tightly plotted structures (fig. 14). In Italy, where the influence

FIG. 13. *Bicycle Thief* (1948), directed by Vittorio De Sica. Generally regarded as the masterpiece of the neo-realist movement, De Sica's film was more concerned with posing questions than with providing easy answers.

FIG. 14. *Umberto D* (1952), directed by Vittorio De Sica. Like Rossellini, De Sica often used non-professional actors in his films, even in leading roles. The principals in *Shoeshine, Bicycle Thief,* and *Umberto D* were all non-professionals.

of neo-realism remained strongest, Federico Fellini and Michelangelo Antonioni gradually broke away from the political and documentary biases of the movement in order to pursue more personal and subjective themes, but significantly, neither director bothered very much with plots. Mood and character dominated their works.

In a sense, this rejection of plot in favor of character, atmosphere, and ideas was hardly a novelty in European artistic circles. After Joyce, Proust, and Faulkner, the novel clearly was heading in non-narrative directions. With the dominance of abstract expressionism in the visual arts, anecdotal subject matter—or indeed, any recogniseable "content"—was similarly rejected in painting and sculpture. Even the theater, perhaps the most conservative of the arts, had come around to de-emphasing plots. As far back as 1900, Chekhov's delicate elegies seemed to have done away with the very "soul" of drama—Aristotle's concept of narrative action. In Europe, there had been a long tradition of accepting films as a serious art form. Consequently, when film-makers began de-emphasising plots in their movies, European intellectuals viewed the move as a shift into the main cultural stream.

In America, however, films had long been considered a staple of the entertainment industry, even by our best directors. Consequently, the influence of neo-realism was predictably small in the Forties and Fifties. Like the great Victorian novelists, the best American directors—Ford, Huston, Lang, Welles, Hitchcock—remained primarily story-tellers. Most of their greatest achievements in this period were in compactly plotted *genre* films—the western, the thriller, the *film noir*. Cinematic excellence in Hollywood was still based on production values, star appeal, and—most of all— "good stories." If European intellectuals admired these films for their "artistic" elements, so much the better, but generally these qualities were in addition to, not instead of, a strong story line.

Elia Kazan was one of the few major American directors of this period to be influenced by neo-realism, particularly in the use of authentic urban locations, the use of non-professional actors (though primarily for minor roles), and in the development of explicit sociopolitical themes (fig. 15). Significantly, Kazan's movies (*Boomerang, Panic in the Streets, On the Waterfront, A Face in the Crowd*) did not eschew plots—the "new look" of his films was largely confined to matters of detail, not to structure.

Occasionally, even *genre* directors were influenced by neo-realism. Samuel Fuller's excellent *Steel Helmet,* for example, attempts to suggest the endlessness of the Korean war by dipping into the story at an apparently arbitrary moment. We are introduced to the protagonist

Alice's Restaurant *and the Tradition of the Plotless Film* 151

FIG. 15. *On the Waterfront* (1954), directed by Elia Kazan. Kazan's film blended two *genres* — the gangster film and the urban documentary — with surprising success. Many of the minor characters were played by non-professional actors.

after his outfit has been wiped out by a Communist military ambush. At the conclusion of the film (after another outfit has been virtually destroyed), Fuller adds the title: "This Story Has No End." Despite the apparent influence of neo-realism and its open-ended structures, however, Fuller's film is typical, in most respects, of its *genre*, and observes most of the action-oriented conventions of battle movies.

For a decade or so, the cinema settled into three discernible niches: the "art" film, dominated by the *avant-garde* and the neo-realists (mostly Europeans and the Japanese); the "commercial" film, dominated primarily by American *genre* directors (figs. 16, 17, 18); and what might be called the "genteel" or "prestige" film, a curious mixture of serious subjects and conventional techniques. Like the commerical film-makers, the directors of genteel movies worked within the framework of narrative structures, though dialogue plays a very important role, far more so than in most *genre* films. The characters in such movies generally discuss ideas in an explict manner.

Virtually all the major British movies of this period fall into the prestige category, as do a number of American films. (Typical movies:

FIG. 16. *Man Hunt* (1941), directed by Fritz Lang.

FIG. 17. *Notorious* (1946), directed by Alfred Hitchcock.

Alice's Restaurant *and the Tradition of the Plotless Film*

FIG. 18. *Key Largo* (1948), directed by John Huston. The majority of American films in the Forties were still tightly-plotted *genre* films—spy thrillers, suspense films, *films noirs*. These were the works that most impressed the French New Wave critic-directors in the Fifties, the films they championed in polemical article after article.

William Wyler's *The Best Years of Our Lives* and *Friendly Persuasion;* Kazan's *Pinky* and *Gentlemen's Agreement;* Fred Zinnemann's *Teresa, The Search*, and *A Hatful of Rain;* and most of the films of producer-director Stanley Kramer.) In France, the genteel tradition was dominated by René Clément, André Cayatte, and Claude Autant-Lara. Directors of this kind of film tackled important social themes, though the treatment of the themes was often heavy-handed and sometimes equivocal. Many of these movies were dominated by mildly leftish screenwriters rather than their directors, and one of the most unfortunate aspects of this literary domination is the tendency of many of the characters to spout rather artificial speeches (often out of character) which were intended to be "inspirational" to the audience. At the time, these films were frequently hailed by cinematically naive intellectuals as great works of art. Invariably, such adjectives as "mature," "serious," and "distinguished" were used to describe them. Today they're generally (and sometimes unfairly) thought to be fundamentally dishonest and artistically bland. At best, they are patronised as "sincere."

Then, in the final years of the Fifties in France, an extraordinary synthesis took place. The high and low roads of the art and commerical movies merged, while the middle road of genteel liberalism was contemptuously dismissed. In the polemical journal *Cahiers du Cinéma,* a number of aggressive young critics (many soon to turn to film-making) wrote enthusiastically of the virtues of the American *genre* tradition. Truffaut, Godard, Claude Chabrol, and Eric Rohmer, among others, championed American *genre* films for their energy, economy, and narrative brilliance. Their heroes: John Ford (fig. 19), Howard Hawks, Fritz Lang, Samuel Fuller, and Alfred Hitchcock. Also—somewhat disconcertingly—Jean Renoir and Roberto Rossellini. Truffaut, and in collaboration, Rohmer and Chabrol, wrote books on Hitchcock and his films. They were particularly lavish in their praise of Hitchcock's

FIG. 19. *Stagecoach* (1939), directed by John Ford. Ford was much admired by Truffaut and Godard, who responded not only to the spectacular beauty of the American's works, but also to his simple humanist values.

FIG. 20. *Psycho* (1960), directed by Alfred Hitchcock. Perhaps more than any other American director, Hitchcock was the reigning favorite with the *Cahiers du Cinéma* critics, who explicated his works with sometimes over-ingenious zeal.

precise, economical plots—in which every shot is calculated to contribute to the relentless unfolding of a human destiny (fig. 20). Undaunted by the traditionally *déclassé* status of the suspense thriller, these critics recognised no intrinsic inferiority in this *genre* and no sooner would criticise Hitchcock for using its conventions than they would Shakespeare for employing them in *Macbeth*.

The documentary and lyric traditions of Rossellini and Renoir were to exert a counter tendency in many of the New Wave films. In 1956, Truffaut was even an assistant to Rossellini on several projects, though no films resulted from the association. In 1963, Rossellini helped to write the script to Godard's *Les carabiniers,* which was photographed in a style that was intended as "a homage to Louis Lumière." Truffaut's first feature, *The 400 Blows (Les quatre cent coups,* 1959) seemed to owe more to De Sica and the lyrical films of Jean Vigo than to any American film-maker. *Jules and Jim* (1961) was predominantly Renoirian in its leisurely, elegant lyricism (fig. 21). *Shoot the Piano*

FIG. 21. *Jules and Jim* (1961), directed by François Truffaut. Along with Agnès Varda's *Le bonheur* (1965), Truffaut's film was virtually a homage to the *oeuvre* of Jean Renoir.

Player (1960) was something of a hybrid: its underworld plot was indebted to Hawks, Hitchcock, and Lang while its love scenes could be traced to Renoir. Eventually, Truffaut's movies split into two types: his plotless lyrical films—*Stolen Kisses (Baisers volés), Bed and Board (Domicile conjugale)*– which are in the tradition of Renoir and Rossellini; and his Americanesque *genre* movies—*The Bride Wore Black, Fahrenheit 451, Mississippi Mermaid (La sirène du Mississippi)*. Most critics seem to agree that his richest gifts are lyrical, not narrative (fig. 22). Truffaut needs room to move around, and plots have a way of constricting his spontaneity and ease.

Despite their obvious borrowings and "homages" to American directors, then, the New Wave film-makers modified the conventions of the *genre* film considerably. Their movies are more philosophical and intellectual, despite their action-oriented plots (fig. 23, 24). Violence, anxiety and melodrama are used in overtly symbolic ways. Indeed, Godard eventually came to portray gratuitous violence as the perfect symbolic embodiment of contemporary capitalism. After the mid-Sixties, his movies became militantly plotless. He dismissed the very concept of narrative continuity as "reactionary."

FIG. 22. *Stolen Kisses* (1968), directed by François Truffaut. Beginning with *The 400 Blows* (1959), Truffaut made four semi-autobiographical lyrical films, all starring the ubiquitous Jean-Pierre Léaud.

FIG. 23. *Scarface* (1932), directed by Howard Hawks. A great favorite with Godard, Hawks's film is violent, terse, and tough —all the qualities Godard tried to capture in *Breathless*.

FIG. 24. *Breathless* (1959), directed by Jean-Luc Godard. Even in his first feature, Godard was obsessed with cars—especially American cars. This obsession reached its zenith in *Weekend,* which features a seven-minute tracking shot of a monumental traffic jam on a highway.

Godard did not, however, abandon the theme of violence. Indeed, his obsession with violence took on a nightmarish intensity. Without plots to "make sense" of the screaming, the slugging, the brutal killings, and the terrifying auto crashes, his films seemed as chaotically fragmented as the collapsing civilisation he was trying to reflect. In *Weekend* (1967), for example, he presents a world of such pointless cruelty and destruction, the characters hardly bother to notice anymore. Godard's rejection of plot was both a political and an artistic decision, for he recognised that a sequential narrative was an inappropriate vehicle for his political themes. Plots tend to suggest causes and effects. cohesion, meaningful actions and inter-actions; but Godard's point is that these qualities are absent in capitalist societies. The "incoherent" plots are used metaphorically, reflecting in kind the incoherence of contemporary life. Godard has been accused by critics of committing the "mimetic fallacy"—of conveying a characteristic by reproducing it literally. Under sensitive analysis, however, his best movies bear up structurally. They are no more literally incoherent than Chekhov's plays dealing with boredom are literally boring, though both artists would insist upon the validity of an audience's experiencing at least a degree of what is being conveyed.

Godard rejected plots for yet another reason: his best films deal with young people attempting to discover who they are, searching for a sense of purpose and a coherent set of values. In attempting to create a counter culture to replace the traditional values the young people have rejected, they often seem fickle and even brutal. What Godard is trying to capture, however, is the tentative existential groping of the young people in their efforts to create cohesion from chaos. He forces us to experience how very hard it is to grow up decently in a world gone mad. From the rubbish heap of contemporary life, they must sort out what's valuable, reject what's dehumanising. At the age of eighteen or twenty these distinctions are not always apparent. Hence the improvised, whimsical episodes, the "false leads" that seem to go nowhere in Godard's movies. In effect, he insists upon the relevance of every "irrelevance"—like the neo-realists, he prefers organic structures to preconceived neat formulas. He refuses to exploit the advantages of hindsight.

Although he was not a particularly good critic, Godard demonstrates in his movies that he is a great film historian. In a sense, his films are a summation of the entire spectrum of movie history. The sheer breadth of his techniques and styles is astonishing. Within one film, he will combine the lyrical spontaneity of Renoir, the politically oriented excavation of social facts of the neo-realists, the exploitation of chance and accident of the *cinéma-vérité* documentarists, the stylised poetic images of Jean Cocteau and other *avant-garde* film-makers, and the hyper-activity of American *genre* films. Who else but Godard would make a "neo-realist musical" (!) like the whimsically bizzarre *A Woman Is a Woman (Une femme est une femme)?* In this film he combines the elements of the M-G-M musicals of Vincente Minnelli (which he loves), with the "dailiness" of Rossellini's neo-realist masterpieces (which he also loves). Who else but Godard? Because of him, the cinema will never be quite the same. Even Ingmar Bergman, in *The Shame* and *The Passion of Anna,* abandoned—at least temporarily — the theatrically structured, artfully crafted films on which his international reputation rested (figs. 25, 26, 27).

Although Godard's movies have never been great commercial successes in the U.S.A., it was only a matter of time before Godardism — and particularly the plotless film—was imported to America. The old masters—Ford, Hitchcock, Lang, Hawks—were aging, and their imitators were merely repeating *genre* formulas soullessly, at least for the

FIG. 25. *The Seventh Seal* (1956), directed by Ingmar Bergman.

FIG. 26. *The Shame* (1968), directed by Ingmar Bergman.

FIG. 27. *The Passion of Anna* (1970), directed by Ingmar Bergman. Though Bergman claims to dislike Godard's films, his influence — either direct or indirect — can be seen in the Swede's more recent films. Prior to the debut of the New Wave, most of Bergman's movies were rather theatrical, with an emphasis on stylised lighting, closed forms, and pictorial beauty. After the early Sixties, Bergman's films began to change, with a new "documentary" (Godardian?) look; open forms, fast stock, hand-held shots, interview scenes, Brechtian endistancing techniques, extremely long takes, jump-cuts and an emphasis on more political themes.

most part. Perhaps it was inevitable that talented younger directors would turn to Europe for inspiration. Spurred by the examples of Godard, Antonioni and Resnais, virtually all the major European film-makers (though in varying degrees) were abandoning tight narratives. It's difficult to assign a beginning point to the plotless film in the U.S.A., though some critics might point to Dennis Hopper's lyrical *Easy Rider*. Of the plotless movies produced here since the mid-Sixties, however, Arthur Penn's *Alice's Restaurant* is perhaps the most strikingly Godardian, and itself something of a summation of the history of the plotless film, though of course it's doubtful that Penn had this in mind when he made the movie.

III

When *Alice's Restaurant* first opened in the U.S.A. it met with a popular reception, and a fairly warm critical response, though virtually all the critics and reviewers expressed reservations about its "formlessness" and "lack of structure." Strangely enough, even Pauline Kael, who had responded with enthusiasm to Penn's previous *Bonnie and Clyde* (which Godard originally was to have directed) was disappointed that *Alice's Restaurant* seemed to lack a central idea.[4] Her reaction to the film's ambiguity and plotlessness is especially puzzling in light of the fact that she is one of Godard's most sensitive and astute admirers.

In fact, *Alice's Restaurant* is a good deal more unified than most of Godard's work, for it employs as its principle of cohesion one of the oldest of metaphors—the journey *motif*. Roads—both literal and symbolic—connect the various episodes in a loose, flexible structure that emphasises the concept of parallelism. Somewhat in the manner of Renoir, these road *motifs* are varied musically: one character's "journey" is juxtaposed with another's, and so on throughout the film (fig. 28). What is important is not so much the *sequence* of journeys, but their thematic inter-relationships. The main "traveler" in the film is Arlo Guthrie, who narrates the story on the soundtrack. In a symbolic sense, Arlo's tentative groping toward maturity, or his "thing," as he calls it, is one of the major journeys of the movie.

The road *motif* is introduced at the very beginning of the film, when we see Arlo hitch-hiking his way to college, where he has enrolled in order to avoid the draft. After he drops out of school, we again see him on the road, hitch-hiking home. Along the way, he is dropped off near a revivalist meeting tent late at night, where Arlo observes on the soundtrack, "I guess Woody's road ran through here sometime," thus establishing a parallel between his "journey" and his father's. There are a number of shots of Arlo on the road between New York, where his parents live, and Stockbridge, Massachusetts, where Alice and Ray have their church. Significantly, in one of these road sequences, Arlo is trapped in an Army convoy of trucks and jeeps—a visual reminder of the threat of military conscription which looms above his head.

Arlo's "road" is essentially linear, though it zig-zags somewhat from college to New York to Massachusetts, and finally back to New

---

4. See her brief commentary in "The Bottom of the Pit," *The New Yorker* (September 27, 1969), p. 127.

FIG. 28. *Alice's Restaurant* (1969), directed by Arthur Penn. Like the works of Godard, Penn's movies are filled with vehicles—a visual reminder of the mobile life-styles preferred by many of their characters.

York again. This relative linearity suggests the fairly uncomplicated development of a stable, mature young man. He encounters stumbling blocks from time to time, but in most cases these obstacles are placed in Arlo's way by outside institutions. Some of the obstacles are due to self-doubts as well, which is perfectly natural for a young man in his late teens. In a scene between him and Woody in the hospital for example, Arlo explains to his dying father his sudden sense of anxiety at being exempted from the draft: "Now that they're not after me to do what I don't want to do, what *do* I want to do? May take me some hard traveling to find that out."[5]

As Robin Wood has shown in his excellent study, *Arthur Penn*,[6]

---

5. *Alice's Restaurant*, a Screenplay by Venable Herndon and Arthur Penn (New York: Doubleday & Company, 1970), p. 121.
6. Published in New York by Frederick A. Praeger, Inc., in 1970.

most of Penn's protagonists are outsiders of some sort, beginning with the outlaw Billy the Kid in *The Left-Handed Gun* (1957), Penn's first movie. Both Annie Sullivan and Helen Keller in *The Miracle Worker* (1962) are outsiders by virtue of their physical abnormalities (fig. 29). In *Mickey One* (1964), the sleazy night-club comedian Mickey is ruthlessly persecuted by anonymous conspirators (fig. 30). Sheriff Calder in *The Chase* (1965) is virtually the only decent man in a town deranged by violence (fig. 31). *Bonnie and Clyde* (1967) features two outlaws as protagonists (fig. 32), and Penn's *Little Big Man* (1970) deals with a renegade white man who is brought up by Indians, but doesn't really fit in with either white or Indian societies (fig. 33). Arlo Guthrie is no exception to this pattern. As a long-hair, he is clearly outside the mainstream of America's dominant culture. Only at the hippie church of Alice and Ray does Arlo fit in, for this is the only community where he can share the values and life-style of his fellows.

Penn emphasises Arlo's outsider status through a number of visual

FIG. 29. *The Miracle Worker* (1962), directed by Arthur Penn. Adapted from a stage play, Penn's second feature now strikes him as too stagey, though he still likes the violent scenes between Annie (Anne Bancroft) and Helen (Patty Duke).

FIG. 30. *Mickey One* (1965), directed by Arthur Penn. Penn's first totally independent film (he produced as well as directed) was not very successful either critically or commercially. Most viewers found its symbolism and allegorical structure self-conscious.

FIG. 31. *The Chase* (1966), directed by Arthur Penn. Scripted by Lillian Hellman (who later repudiated the finished product), *The Chase* was badly butchered by the executives at Columbia Pictures, who cut out entire chunks from the film. Robin Wood considers the work—despite its choppy continuity—Penn's first "indisputable masterpiece."

FIG. 32. *Bonnie and Clyde* (1967), directed by Arthur Penn. Penn's greatest commercial and critical success is perhaps his most Godardian movie, filled with violence, comedy, sudden shifts in tone, and a profound sense of ambivalence.

FIG. 33. *Little Big Man* (1971), directed by Arthur Penn. Like many of Penn's movies, this is essentially a *genre* film, yet with a characteristic twist in its treatment. In many ways, the film mocks its predecessors, especially the westerns of John Ford.

motifs, primarily doors and windows. These images tend to define a discrete community in the film, a cohesive set of values which Arlo doesn't or cannot share. These cultural communities are strung out like wayside stations along the various "roads" of the film. From Arlo's point of view, they often seem like so many hostile armed camps which he must circumvent on his journey to self-identity.

Arlo's outsider status is certainly apparent in the provincial town where his college is located. The hostility of the townspeople is so great that he's thrown through a plate glass window of a pizza parlor. The camera photographs the act from outside the window in the street. In the college itself, his music professor explodes at him for playing "folk junk" instead of "serious" music. The conclusion of the scene is also photographed from outside the large window of the music room in the corridor. (Throughout the film, Penn uses corridors as variations of his road *motif.*) Through the music room window, we see the furious professor pointing the way out to Arlo, accompanied by the exasperated exclamation, "You are utterly devoid of musical talent!"

A less hysterical example of Arlo's outsider status takes place at the revival tent. Here, the values of the community are defined by the fundamentalist Christian faith of the congregation. The scene is presented sympathetically, ending with the hymn, "Amazing Grace," which becomes a thematic *motif* in the film. Significantly, Arlo stays well outside the tent—an interested observer, but an outsider nonetheless. The camera photographs the scene from behind Arlo in a long shot, dollying to the right as he travels along his separate road. This scene jump-cuts to a darkened landing in a subway station, where Arlo climbs up the steps into the light of New York City. This tunnel image in turn leads to images of corridors in the hospital where his father, Woody Guthrie, lies seriously ill.

Arlo's relationship with his parents is portrayed as a fine one — affectionate, mutually tolerant, flexible (fig. 34). Even with his parents however, Arlo is an outsider, a visitor. His mother seldom ventures outside the door of the hospital room, and when she does it is only so far as the corridor. Arlo's mother accepts the fact that he must travel his "own road." The images of doors and corridors reinforce this essential separation, as does the editing, which often emphasises close-ups (isolation) rather than the more communal long shot.

Doors, windows and corridors are also prominent in the Army physical scene, where the tone of the film becomes openly farcical (fig. 35). Perhaps this is the most extreme instance of Arlo's outsider status. Significantly, he remains outside the Army because of his "criminal status" as a litterer. As in *The Chase,* Penn emphasises the ironies of a protagonist trying to live decently in a society where acceptablity is

FIG. 34. *Alice's Restaurant*. Music is one of the bridges of communication throughout the film. In one hospital sequence, Arlo plays a lively duet with folksinger Pete Seeger.

defined by one's enthusiasm for violence and destruction: in *Alice's Restaurant,* the Vietnamese war is always hovering in the background.

Arlo seems to find his "thing" at the church community of Alice and Ray. Significantly, the first time we see him there, Arlo stands under the arched doorway of the church. This time, however, the camera photographs him from *within* the room, not outside of it. Alice and Ray welcome him like loving parents reunited with a prodigal son. When Ray proclaims that the church is a place "to be the way we want to be," Alice asks, "What more do we need?" Playfully, Arlo answers, "Amazing grace." The throwaway line acquires more ironic resonance as the film progresses. During most of the movie, Arlo is at home with Alice and Ray, who indeed are virtually surrogate parents for most of the youngsters. But eventually they leave the roost, and even Arlo sees that he does not really belong here. His "thing" is linked with Mari-Chan, his girl (fig. 36), not with the hippie church community, which he implicitly rejects at the end of the movie.

In the manner of several of Renoir's films, Penn's movie parallels

Alice's Restaurant *and the Tradition of the Plotless Film*

FIG. 35. *Alice's Restaurant*. The army physical sequence is brilliantly satirical, filled with visual humor and witty spoofs on traditional pre-induction rituals.

three different age groups, each with different sets of values. The youngest are in their late teens and early twenties, and are represented primarily by Arlo and Shelly. The oldest are in late middle-age. The major characters in this generation—Woody and Marjorie Guthrie,

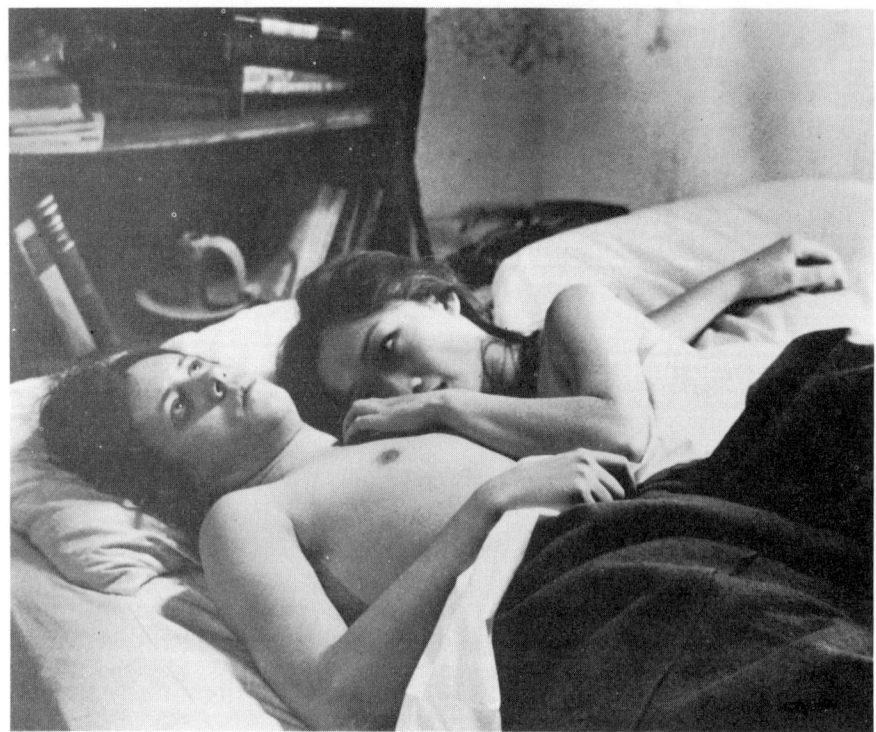

FIG. 36. *Alice's Restaurant*. Arlo and Mari-Chan in their artist-loft in New York. He tells her, "All of a sudden I feel in a hurry to find out what my thing's going to be. Who. And where."

Pete Seeger, and Ruth, the night-club owner—were in "the Movement" in the Thirties (fig.37). The "aging children," Alice and Ray, are in a kind of transitional generation: they share many of the values and the liberated life-style of the youngsters, yet like the middle-aged characters, Alice and Ray need more structure to their lives. In effect, the Brocks are trapped between two worlds, and are not totally at home in either. Penn's treatment of these three groups is almost classically symmetrical in its balance. We see the weaknesses and strengths of each. Indeed, one of the principal reasons Penn made the film was because he was offended by many of the *clichés* about the "youth culture" in other contemporary films:

> Some movies are creating the myths of the young. They promote the notion that freedom from all authority is an unqualified good, that mobility as a life-style is superior to permanence, that the older generation is totally corrupt, that cool is the only legitimate emotional response. And what's worse about these films is that they patronize young people. They reduce

Alice's Restaurant *and the Tradition of the Plotless Film*

FIG. 37. *Alice's Restaurant.* After lending Arlo some money, Ruth makes a sexual advance toward him; he in turn rebuffs her rather crudely.

them to their accouterments—their grass, their bikes, their music—all their labels[7]

In *Alice's Restaurant*, it's a form of spiritual and psychological serenity—"amazing grace"—that confers happiness and emotional stability, not a lifestyle *per se*. Nor is this serenity confined to the members of one generation. Arlo's easy-going good humor is countered by Shelly's addiction to heroin; the humane idealism of the Old Left (more alluded to than shown) of Seeger, Woody, and Marjorie is contrasted with the sexual opportunism of Ruth; and Alice's quasi-maternal warmth and sensitivity (fig. 38) are countered by Ray's childish egocentricity (fig. 39).

Like many of the best works of Godard, Penn's film is constantly qualified by a sense of ambivalence, though Penn is a far more sympathetic and warm director, even with characters he doesn't admire.

---

7. Quoted in "The New Movies," *Newsweek* (December 7, 1970), p. 72.

FIG. 38. *Alice's Restaurant*. Throughout the film, Alice acts as mother, friend, and defender to Shelly—but eventually the sexual attraction between them is too great and they become lovers.

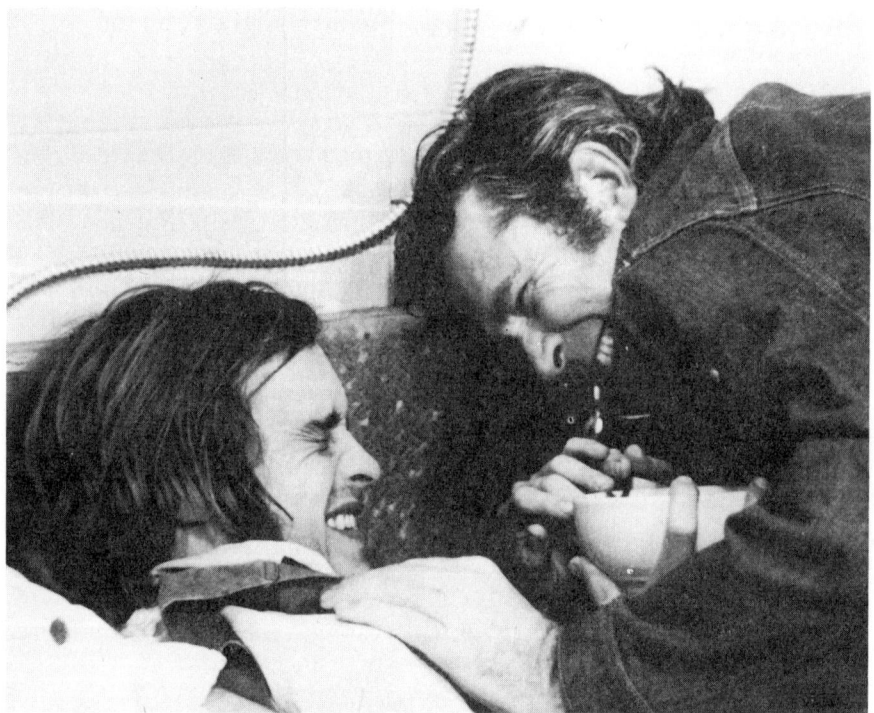

FIG. 39. *Alice's Restaurant*. Ray's relationship with Shelly is also constantly shifting. Sometimes Ray acts like an outraged father, other times (as here) like a fellow goof-off, and still others like a jealous husband. Ultimately these ambiguities prove too much for Shelly to handle.

Alice's Restaurant *and the Tradition of the Plotless Film*

With an almost documentary insistence on truthfuless, he does not take cheap pot-shots at the alternate communities (except for the Army). The Episcopalians who previously owned the Trinity Church are portrayed as dignified, and sincerely sorrowful at the loss of their

FIG. 40. *Alice's Restaurant*. One of the most amusing sequences in the film is the "Alice's Restaurant Massacree," based on Arlo's original recording, in which he and his friend Geoff are arrested by Officer Obie for littering.

church. "Straight" characters are not dimissed as fools. Officer Obie, for example, is one of the most likable and appealing characters in the film (fig. 40). There are even a few episodes where radically different cultures seem compatible, generally those scenes centered on a community ritual of some kind, like the Thanksgiving Day feast and the "wedding" sequence (fig. 41).

Penn concentrates on a number of separate journeys or roads. Arlo's is the most apparent, for it forms the structural spine of the film; but Shelly (a parallel figure to Arlo) and Ray and Alice are also portrayed as journeyers. The roads of Shelly and Ray are essentially circular, for they are associated with the motorcyle racing track. (Significantly, Arlo is not a participant in the race.) The symbolism of the circular track is appropriate, for both men lack a specific goal, and lapse into repetitive behavior cycles (fig. 42). Shelly returns to his heroin habit (thus endangering the existence of the entire church community), and the last we see of him he is riding his motorcycle desperately into the blackness of the night. His "road" leads ultimately to death.

FIG. 41. *Alice's Restaurant.* The early part of the wedding sequence is primarily photographed in long shots, which emphasize the communal aspects of the event, with many people sharing the same frame.

FIG. 42. *Alice's Restaurant*. The racing scene. Alice's main problem is her inability to help everyone without hurting someone. At one point she says: "Guess I'm the bitch who had too many pups, and just couldn't take them all milking me."

Ray's behavior is also cyclical. After Alice leaves him, he promises to change, to be less selfish and thoughtless (fig. 43). The final sequence, however, clearly shows that Ray hasn't changed at all. It is also Ray who suggests that he and Alice marry again, this time with an elaborate ceremony to re-cement their relationship. But again, the final sequence emphasises the probable disintegration of their marriage. Ray wants to "start over" with another experimental community, this time on a farm in Vermont where they will have more space. But everyone—except Ray—recognises that the failure of the church community was due to spiritual and psychological shortcomings, not physical. (Ray is consistently characterised in physical terms: psychologically, he is the least self-aware character in the film.)

Alice's "journey" is inextricably bound with Ray's, though she is portrayed as far more sensitive to the pitfalls of their joint venture. Closely associated with the central *motif* of roads is the idea of time, and particularly time's passing. As a very young man, Arlo can afford to experiment leisurely on his road to self-realisation. Alice and Ray are in their thirties, however, and unlike the young people, they need

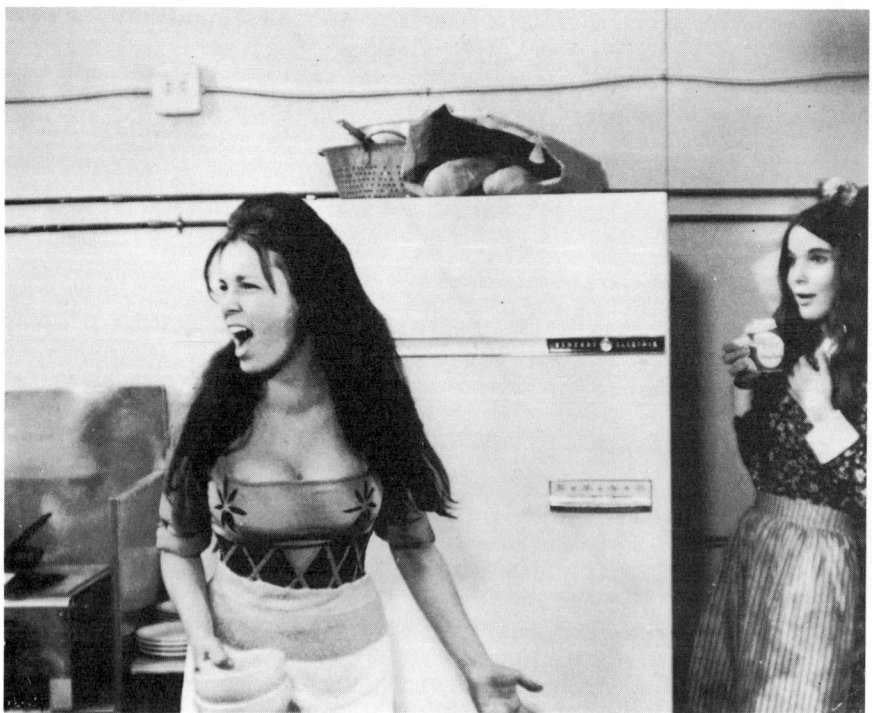

FIG. 43. *Alice's Restaurant*. Alice explodes at Ray and Shelly. Throughout the film, it is she who invariably gets stuck with the dirty work, with the adult responsibilities, while Ray clowns with the youngsters.

more stability and permanence in their lives—or at least Alice does. Time however is running out, a fact emphasised in the sequence of Shelly's funeral. The bleak snow-covered cemetary is photographed primarily in long shot, with isolated couples and individuals standing forlornly in the snow among the tombstones (fig. 44). In one shot, the camera slowly travels down the road at the edge of the cemetary, while Joni Mitchell's melancholy "Songs to Aging Children" can be heard on the soundtrack. The time-consuming dolly shot, combined with the road *motif* and the lyrics of the song all emphasise the theme of time's passage. Seldom have image, sound and movement combined to produce an effect of such overwhelming poignance.

Penn repeats this technical combination in the final sequence of the film. Most of the wedding guests have gone home. In a drunken flight of fancy, Ray talks of selling the church and starting over again in Vermont. No one really listens, except Alice, who gradually begins to realise that nothing has changed. He tries to persuade Arlo and Mari-

Alice's Restaurant *and the Tradition of the Plotless Film*

FIG. 44. *Alice's Restaurant*. The cemetary sequence. With the death of Shelly, Alice and Ray—who both feel that they failed the boy in some way—ponder seriously what they have become, how they have failed their dream.

Chan to stay, but they too leave (fig. 45). Ray stumbles back into the church, leaving Alice standing outside the church door, her hair garlanded with flowers, her wedding dress slightly crumpled. As she looks past the camera, her face reflects an ambiguous mixture of anxiety and desolation. Never has she seemed so totally alone and vulnerable. On the soundtrack, the cheery lyrics of Arlo's title song ("You can get anything you want at Alice's Restaurant") are distorted into a bitter ironic mockery by the use of an echo chamber. As the song continues, the camera dollys to the left, while occasional intervening tree trunks obliterate our view of her. A cloud slowly snuffs out the bright sunlight, and she is surrounded in a grayish semi-darkness. As the camera dollys out to the left, it also zooms in slowly to the right, producing an eerie sense of movement toward and away from Alice simultaneously. The dolly movement—like the previous cemetary shot—tends to suggest the idea of time's passing and the impermanence of things. The slow zooming in suggests Alice's gradual realisation that the quality of

FIG. 45. *Alice's Restaurant*. The wedding sequence. Like Alice, Arlo and Mari-Chan sadly contemplate the failure to form a permanent community. Eventually they leave, to travel their separate road.

her life will not improve, but will probably deteriorate. It is a brilliant shot, charged with bitter and disturbing ambiguities—surely one of the most emotionally resonant moments in the cinema of recent years.

IV

The artistic excellence of *Alice's Restaurant* is hardly open to dispute, but the film is also important historically, for it combines many of the major strands of the essentially European tradition of the plotless film. It shares this distinction with other contemporary American movies, but none of them has blended the traditions of the documentary, the lyrical film, and the New Wave with such compelling authority.

The influence of neo-realism and the documentary tradition can be seen in Penn's use of non-professional actors and authentic locations. Whenever possible, the director used fast stock and available lighting, which give his images a gritty newsreel immediacy. The exploration of the youth culture is far more accurate than anything that could be seen on TV at the time, or read about in most magazines and newspapers. Few films have shown the faces of America with such extraordinary poetic insight. Even the most insignificant extras—like the Episcopalian parishioners—are utterly authentic.

The influence of Renoir and the lyrical tradition can be seen in Penn's use of parallelism and variations on a theme as his structural principle. The sexual scenes are also reminiscent of Renoir, for the characters make love whenever and wherever the impulse seizes them. Penn also integrates music more organically into his film than most contemporary American directors. The lyrics of the three major songs—"Amazing Grace," "Alice's Restaurant," and "Songs to Aging Children"—comment directly on the characters and the theme of the film. The treatment of Officer Obie and the other straight characters also suggests Renoir's warm, sympathetic humanism. His attitude of "every man has his reasons" could just as easily be applied to most of Penn's characters.

His apparent debt to the New Wave directors—and particularly Godard—can be seen in the sudden shifts of tone. Penn flips audaciously from comedy (Arlo's commentary, the restaurant scenes) to tragedy (Shelly's addiction and death) to lyricism (the communal scenes, the love scenes) to slapstick farce (the Keystone cops routine at the garbage site). Indeed, Penn has expressed some misgivings about the "Alice's Restaurant Massacree" sequence, which is based on Arlo's original recording and served as the initial inspiration for the movie.[8] Penn feels that the tone of this sequence is too farcical, too out of keeping with the rest of the film. Most audiences would probably disagree. Dede Allen's excellent elliptical editing also seems indebted to the New Wave, particularly in its frequent use of jump-cuts.

Penn's reputation is largely based on his genius in portraying violence, and though *Alice's Restaurant* is a gentle, almost elegiac film, it contains a number of scenes that are as exciting and action-oriented as any American *genre* movie: Arlo's fight in the pizza parlor; the motorcycle racing scenes; and especially the sequence in the church, when Shelly is brought back in handcuffs by Officer Obie, who has arrested him for pushing and possession of heroin (fig. 46). The ambivalent treatment of subject matter is a hallmark of Godard's best films, as well as the deliberate fragmentation of narrative continuity. In these respects Penn's film seems virtually a homage to Godard.

---

8. See Wood, pp. 98-99.

FIG. 46. *Alice's Restaurant*. One of the most visually stunning — and violent — sequences in the film is when Office Obie brings Shelly back to the church in handcuffs. The youth has returned to his heroin habit, probably out of frustration for his hopeless attraction to Alice.

INDEX

Accident, 106-7
African Queen, The, 67
Alice's Restaurant, 15, 23, 71, 72, 98, 132-60 passim, 161-80
Allegory 118-20, 165
Allen, Dede, 179
All Fall Down, 114
Alphaville, 20, 115
Andersson, Bibi, 125, 128, 131
Antonioni, Michelangelo, 81-82, 83, 103, 116, 133, 150, 161
Arnheim, Rudolf, 91-92, 93, 101.
Autant-Lara, Claude, 153
Avant-garde, 20, 151, 159
Avventura, L', 81-82, 83

Bancroft, Anne, 71, 106, 164
Bardot, Brigitte, 34, 56
Barr, Charles, 15, 99
Bazin, André, 65-67, 69, 89
Beatty, Warren, 114
Beauty and the Beast, 116
Bed and Board, 156
Before the Revolution, 85-88
Belmondo, Jean-Paul, 22, 56
Bergman, Ingmar, 44, 49, 95, 107-8, 113, 120, 125-31, 159-61
Bertolucci, Bernardo, 41, 85-88
Best Years of Our Lives, The, 153
Bicycle Thief, 146, 149
Billard, Pierre (and Robert Hughes), 39, 45, 47
Birds, The, 24
Blonde Venus, 108

Blood of a Poet, 54, 90, 117
Blue Angel, The, 14
Bluestone, George, 89, 90, 91, 94
Bogarde, Dirk, 106
Bogart, Humphrey, 67
Bogdanovich, Peter, 112
Bonheur, Le, 156
Bonnie and Clyde, 162, 164, 166
Boomerang, 150
Boorman, John, 112
Bordwell, David, 15
Boudu Saved from Drowning, 141, 144-45
Breathless, 22, 25, 36, 53, 75, 157, 158
Brecht, Bertolt, 27-28, 44, 50, 135, 161
Bride Wore Black, The, 46, 156
Bruckman, Clyde, 61
Buñuel, Luis, 105
Butch Cassidy and the Sundance Kid, 106

Cahiers du Cinéma, 154, 155
Carabiniers, Les, 57, 155
Cassavetes, John, 111, 113, 137
Cayatte, André, 153
Chabrol, Claude, 154
Chaplin, Charles, 14, 132
Chase, The, 164, 165, 167
Chayevsky, Paddy, 87-88
Chinoise, La, 2, 20, 50, 53, 54, 56, 74
Cinéma Vérité, 27, 159
Citizen Kane 83-84, 101, 106, 113-14, 118
Clair, René, 56
Clayton, Jack, 71, 106
Clément, René, 153

Clockwork Orange, A, 70
Cocteau, Jean, 54, 90, 105, 115, 116-17, 159
Contempt, 25, 56
Cops, 60-62
Countess from Hong Kong, A, 14
Coutard, Raoul, 45, 46, 73, 75
Crisp, Donald, 62

Debord, Michael, 31
Deliverance, 112
Deneuve, Catherine, 95
De Sica, Vittorio, 84, 146, 149, 155
Devil is a Woman, The, 14
Doctor Zhivago, 94
Documentary, 20, 26, 46, 58, 135, 136, 137-40, 146, 148, 151, 161, 173, 178
Dreyer, Carl, 21
Duke, Patty, 164
Duport, Catherine-Isabelle, 30
Durgnat, Raymond, 13, 14

Earrings of Madame de ...., The, 80, 106
Easy Rider, 135, 136, 161
Editing, 94-98; editing metaphors, 122, 125, 126, 133, 138, 167
8½, 40, 75-76
Eisenstein, Sergei, 16, 27, 56, 94, 95
Elvira Madigan, 109, 110
Essay: cinematic essay, 19-59
Existential, existentialist, 24, 147, 159

Face in the Crowd, A, 150
Faces, 111, 113, 137
Fahrenheit 451, 156
Farber, Stephen, 15
Feeling and Form, 134-35
Fellini, Fredrico, 40, 75-76, 92, 120, 150
Film as Art, 91
Five Easy Pieces, 135
Flaherty, Robert, 138-40
Fonda, Henry, 68
Fonda, Jane, 97
Ford, John, 16, 81, 132, 150, 154, 159, 166
400 Blows, The, 155, 157
Frame, 15, 16, 37, 49, 61, 62, 64, 76, 82, 84, 98, 101, 102, 103, 104, 121, 129, 142, 174
Frankenheimer, John, 74-75, 114
Friendly Persuasion, 153
Fuller, Samuel, 26, 55, 150-51, 154

Gavin, John, 121
General, The, 61
Genre: genre films, 20, 22, 23, 24, 56, 132, 135, 141, 143, 150-55, 156, 159, 166, 179

Gentlemen's Agreement, 153
Gigi, 56
Godard, Jean-Luc, 2, 13, 19-59, 60, 71, 74, 75, 84, 85, 87, 88, 95, 102, 115, 117, 119, 132, 135, 140, 154, 156-61, 162, 166, 171, 179
Goya, Chantal, 33, 75
Grande Illusion, La, 141, 142, 143
Grant, Cary, 66
Griffith, D. W., 70, 115, 132, 136
Guthrie, Arlo, 162-80 *passim*
Guthrie, Woody, 163, 167, 169, 171

Hamlet, 14, 103, 104
Hard Day's Night, A, 105
Hatful of Rain, A, 153
Hathaway, Henry, 105, 106
Hawks, Howard, 22, 55, 154, 156, 157, 159
Hayworth, Rita, 104
Hellman, Lillian, 165
Hepburn, Katharine, 67, 111
Herndon, Venable, 163
Hill, George Roy, 106
Hiller, Arthur, 87-88
Hitchcock, Alfred, 16, 22, 24, 25, 27, 32, 49, 56, 66, 68-69, 71, 96, 115-16, 118-25, 129, 132, 134, 150, 152, 154, 155, 156, 159
Homage, 44, 55, 56, 156
Hopper, Dennis, 136
Hospital, The, 87-88
Hughes, Robert (and Pierre Billard), 39, 45, 47
Huston, John, 67, 153

Ikiru, 51, 52
Intolerance, 70, 115

Johnson, Ben, 112
Jules and Jim, 44, 46, 72, 73, 155, 156
Juliet of the Spirits, 92

Kael, Pauline, 13, 24, 162
Karina, Anna, 21, 56
Kazan, Elia, 40, 150-51, 153
Keaton, Buster, 60-62, 68
Key Largo, 153
Knack, The, 105
Kracauer, Siegfried, 91
Kramer, Stanley, 153
Kubrick, Stanley, 70, 76-79, 95-96, 108-9
Kurant, Willy, 45
Kurosawa, Akira, 51, 52, 114

Lang, Fritz, 22, 23, 24, 25, 26, 49, 55, 68, 150, 152, 154, 156, 159
Langer, Susanne, 134-35

Index 183

Last Picture Show, The, 112
Last Year at Marienbad, 133
Leacock, Richard, 27
Lean, David, 94
Léaud, Jean-Pierre, 30, 56, 57, 157
Left-Handed Gun, The, 164
Leigh, Janet, 121
Leone, Sergio, 14
Lester, Richard, 96, 105
Letter from an Unknown Woman, 64
Lewis, Jerry, 14
Literature and Film, 89, 98-99
Little Big Man, 164, 166
Long Day's Journey into Night, 79, 109-11
Loren, Sophia, 84
Losey, Joseph, 106-7
Love Story, 74
Lubitsch, Ernst, 56, 71, 93
Lumet, Sidney, 72-74, 78, 96-97, 109-11
Lumière: Louis and Lumière brothers, 137, 140, 155

Macbeth, 102
Magnani, Anna, 145
Magnificent Ambersons, The, 78, 114-15
Manchurian Candidate, The, 74-75
Man Hunt, 23, 152
Marley, John, 111
Marxist, 24, 27, 31, 37, 44, 53, 85, 86, 87, 147
Masculine-Feminine, 15, 19-59, 102
Mason, James, 78
Mastroianni, Marcello, 75
McDowell, Malcolm, 70
Medium Cool, 135
Metaphor, 15, 61, 71-88; metaphoric camera movements, 89-131, 162
Mickey One, 164, 165
Mifune, Toshiro, 114
Miles, Vera, 68, 123
Minnelli, Vincente, 56, 159
Miracle Worker, The, 164
Mise-en-scène: metteur-en-scène, 14, 15, 16, 27, 50-53, 64, 100
Mississippi Mermaid, 156
Mitchell, Joni, 176
Mobile camera, 15, 16, 60-88
Montaigne, Michel, 26, 58-59
Monte Carlo, 93
Moreau, Jeanne, 44
Motif, 68, 69, 75, 82, 83, 85, 94, 105, 106, 118-31 *passim*, 143, 162, 167, 175, 176
Musketeers of Pig Alley, The, 136
My Life to Live, 20, 21, 25

Nanook of the North, 138-39

Navigator, The, 62
Neo-realism, 135, 137, 146-51, 159, 178
Newman, Paul, 106
New Wave, 54, 73, 138-40, 153, 154-61, 178, 179
North by Northwest, 66
Notorious, 152
Novels into Film, 89
Nykvist, Sven, 131

October (Ten Days That Shook the World), 95
Olivier, Laurence, 14, 103
Olvidados, Los, 105
On the Waterfront, 150, 151
Open City, 145, 146, 147-48
Ophüls, Max, 62, 64, 78-81, 82, 106
Orpheus, 105
Othello, 82-83

Paisan, 57, 146
Palance, Jack, 56-57
Pal Joey, 104
Panic in the Streets, 150
Partie de campagne, Une, 140
Pasolini, Pier Paolo, 89
Passion of Anna, The, 113, 159, 161
Paths of Glory, 76-78
Pawnbroker, The, 72-74, 96-97, 109
Peckinpah, Sam, 76, 105
Penn, Arthur, 71, 72, 98, 132-60 *passim*, 161-80
Perkins, Anthony, 121
Persona, 95, 96, 101, 118-19, 125-31
Picnic on the Grass, 140, 144
Pierrot le fou, 26, 117
Pinky, 153
Pinter, Harold, 107
Plaisir, Le, 82
Plot, narrative, 20, 21, 22, 23, 24, 25, 29, 30, 120, 121, 132-80
Polanski, Roman, 94-95, 102
Pollack, Sydney, 97
Psycho, 68-69, 96, 101, 118-25, 130, 133, 142, 155
Pudovkin, Vsevolod, 94, 95
Pumpkin Eater, The, 71, 106

Quinn, Pat, 71

Ramsaye, Terry, 98
Red Desert, 116
Redford, Robert, 106
Renoir, Jean, 26, 135, 138-46, 154, 155, 156, 159, 162, 168, 179

Repulsion, 94-95
Resnais, Alain, 41, 53, 78, 133, 161
Richardson, Ralph, 111
Richardson, Robert, 89, 90, 98-99
Richardson, Tony, 14, 103, 104, 105
Riefenstahl, Leni, 96
Robards, Jason, 111
Rohmer, Eric, 154
Ronde, La, 79
Rossellini, Roberto, 56, 57, 85, 86, 145-50, 154, 155, 156, 159
Roud, Richard, 27, 47
Rules of the Game, The, 141

Saga of Anatahan, The, 14
Saint, Eva Marie, 114
Sarrazin, Michael, 97
Sarris, Andrew, 50, 78-80
Scarface, 22, 55, 157
Scarlet Empress, The, 14, 99, 100
Search, The, 153
Seberg, Jean, 22
Seeger, Pete, 168, 170, 171
See You at Mao, 20, 32
Seventh Seal, The, 120, 160
Shadows, 137
Shame, 107-8, 159, 160
Shoeshine, 146, 149
Shoot the Piano Player, 46, 155-56
Sidney, George, 104
Sight and Sound, 146
Silence, The, 44
Simon, John, 20, 120, 127
Sins of Lola Montès, The, 80
Sirk, Douglas, 14
Sontag, Susan, 20
Stagecoach, 154
Steel Helmet, 150-51
Steiger, Rod, 72, 96
Stockwell, Dean, 111
Stolen Kisses, 156, 157
Strada, La, 120
Strangers on a Train, 121
Strike, 95

Teresa, 153
Terra Trema, La, 146
Testament of Orpheus, 115, 117

Theory of Film, 91
They Shoot Horses Don't They?, 97
Throne of Blood, 114
Through a Glass Darkly, 127
Tom Jones, 105
Topaz, 115-16
Touch of Evil, 111
Triumph of the Will, 96
True Grit, 105
Truffaut, François, 40, 44, 46, 53, 69, 72, 73, 140, 145, 154-57
Two or Three Things I Know About Her, 53
2001: A Space Odyssey, 95-96, 108-9, 135
Two Women, 84

Ullmann, Liv, 125, 128, 131
Umberto, D, 146, 149

Varda, Agnès, 140, 156
Vertigo, 122
Vietnam, 29, 35, 37, 52, 129, 168
Vigo, Jean, 155
Visconti, Luchino, 146
Vitti, Monica, 81
Vladimir and Rosa, 20, 117
Von Sternberg, Josef, 14, 99, 100, 108
Von Sydow, Max, 113

Wagonmaster, 81
Wayne, John, 105
Weekend, 20, 25, 59, 84, 117, 119, 158
Welles, Orson, 41, 49, 78, 82-84, 87, 89, 101, 111, 114-15, 132, 150
Widerberg, Bo, 109, 110
Wild Bunch, The, 76
Wild Child, The, 69, 105
Wild Strawberries, 120
Woman is a Woman, A, 36, 159
Wood, Robin, 15, 120, 125, 127, 163, 165, 179
Woodstock, 135
Wyler, William, 153

You Only Live Once, 23-24, 68

Zabriskie Point, 103, 133
Zavattini, Cesare, 146-50 *passim*
Zinnemann, Fred, 153